MASTERING
TEACHING

Roberta Hestenes
Howard Hendricks
Earl Palmer

MULTNOMAH
Portland, Oregon

Christianity Today, Inc.

Unless otherwise indicated, all Scripture references are from the Holy Bible: New International Version, © 1973, 1978, 1984 by the International Bible Society. Used by permission of Zondervan Bible Publishers.

MASTERING TEACHING
© 1991 by Christianity Today, Inc.
Published by Multnomah Press
Portland, Oregon 97266

Multnomah Press is a ministry of Multnomah School of the Bible, 8435 N.E. Glisan Street, Portland, Oregon 97220.

Printed in the United States of America.

Library of Congress Cataloging-in-Publication Data

Hestenes, Roberta.
    Mastering teaching / Roberta Hestenes, Howard Hendricks, Earl Palmer.
        p.   cm.
    ISBN 0-88070-440-3
    1. Christian education—United States—Teaching methods.
2. Christian education directors—United States.   I. Hendricks, Howard G.   II. Palmer, Earl F.   III. Title.   IV. Series.
BV1534.H45   1991
268'.6—dc20   91-8435
                                                            CIP

91 92 93 94 95 96 97 98 99 - 10 9 8 7 6 5 4 3 2 1

MASTERING
TEACHING

Contents

Introduction

The laying on of hands still warmed my forehead as I called forth the best from those before me, a dozen church school teachers sitting in an amalgam of armchairs and sofas, of clashing eras and patterns, that constituted the church's Fireside Room. I was in my first church, about to fix a not untypical problem: the church school had sagging attendance and low morale. Teachers had lost vision for what they were about.

No problem: I knew what they were about, and I would tell them so in an inspiring lesson at our first teacher training session. So that day I waxed excited:

"It's not *what* you teach but *who* teaches that makes a difference!

"Love is not taught; it's caught!

"Teaching is the key link in Jesus' Great Commission!"

And finally, "Let us consecrate ourselves anew to this holy work, the sacred trust given us by our Lord to instill faith in 'the least of these,' that maturing as disciples, they too may pass the baton of faith to the next generation!"

I scanned what appeared to be awed faces. Silence reigned. One woman raised her hand to acknowledge, I presumed, how inspired she was.

"Mark?"

"Yes, Nancy?" I leaned forward.

"I could really use some craft ideas for first and second graders."

I stared at Nancy, trying to take in her question. Another hand bolted up: "And who is responsible for finding a substitute, the teacher or the church school superintendent? Last year . . ."

"Now wait a minute," interrupted the superintendent. "When I agreed to be superintendent, Mark, you told me I wouldn't have to find substitutes . . ."

From there conversation rapidly descended from the eternal destiny of souls to the location of colored chalk in the supply room.

So much for my first opportunity to oversee the teaching ministry of the church.

Whether it's teaching students or training teachers, few things are more important in ministry than teaching. That business about it being central to the Great Commission is no exaggeration: "Go, therefore, and make disciples of all nations, *teaching* them . . ."

But sometimes our teaching about things inspiring only inspires yawns, and talk about the eternal sometimes degenerates into discussion of the mundane. And some Sunday afternoons we sit alone in the study and wonder: *Is all this making a difference in anyone's daily life?*

We know better, for the Word of God does accomplish something through us and in spite of us. Most days teaching goes well and people seem helped, sometimes moved. But we never leave a class without feeling that this or that could-have gone better. Another challenge always demands our attention.

Our three authors in this volume of Mastering Ministry know these and other challenges of teaching. Better still, they each have learned to meet them successfully.

Howard Hendricks

"We've got a mandate to teach. It's not an option to the church. It's essential. It's not nice; it's necessary. Because the church that ceases to educate, ceases to exist."

It's a warm, fall afternoon, and I sit with Howard Hendricks in his sunlit Dallas Seminary office. His suit coat is off, and his sleeves are rolled up. He's talking about his passion.

"I discovered long ago that teaching is my spiritual gift. And I've spent all of my life fighting to keep people from making me a president or a dean or something. If you take me out of the classroom, I lose my reason for existence."

That's Hendricks: direct, honest, and committed to teaching.

It hasn't always been that way, at least the commitment part. He originally wanted to be a surgeon. He even received a scholarship for premed studies at Northwestern University in Evanston, Illinois. But the summer before he was to enroll, he decided he'd rather become a physician of the soul.

So he entered Wheaton College and began studying for the ministry. Later he earned degrees from Dallas Theological Seminary, where today he is professor of Christian education. He's also director of the Institute of Christian Leadership at Dallas Seminary. He has contributed to dozens of books and journals on the topic of Christian education. His most recent releases are *Teaching to Change Lives* and *Discovering Discipleship* (both Multnomah Press).

Roberta Hestenes

When I attended Fuller Seminary, I took Roberta Hestenes's

class, "Adult Transformation Strategies." Hestenes was thoroughly prepared, engaging, inspiring, and "purpose provoking."

For one assignment, I turned in a series of lesson plans for an adult church school class on "Introduction to the Bible" I was about to teach. I thought my plan for using handouts and class discussion creative, not to mention admirable, until I read her comments. Liberally sprinkled throughout my beautiful lesson plan were remarks like "Why handouts here? What are people going to do with them?" and "Are you sure you want to break into groups at this point?" and "What are you trying to accomplish here?"

I slowly got the point, and in class after class I taught in ministry, I found I was integrating myself in the same way, striving to clarify my purpose and ruthlessly clearing away anything that didn't contribute to it.

Because she gets people to ask themselves the most important questions, Hestenes makes a difference in whatever setting she's in, whether as Bible teacher, professor, or college president. In each setting, she has gotten people to think, to ponder, and eventually to do more for their Lord.

Roberta Hestenes has been president of Eastern College in St. Davids, Pennsylvania since 1987. Prior to that she served as director of adult education at University Presbyterian Church in Seattle, Washington, and then as professor of Christian formation at Fuller Theological Seminary, Pasadena, California. She has also written *Using the Bible in Groups* (Westminster/John Knox).

Earl Palmer

When he preaches, he does word studies from the Greek, and he quotes Dostoevsky and Barth and Bultmann. He's preached a series on The Barmen Declaration, a theological document arising out of 1930s Germany. When we interviewed him, he had just finished teaching a Tuesday morning class on G.K. Chesterton's *Orthodoxy*.

You'd think Earl Palmer is a man with his head in theological clouds. Then again . . .

After Palmer spoke at one seminary chapel, some students

asked their traditional, Reformed preaching professor his opinion of Palmer's preaching.

"He'll do all right," said the professor, "as long as he sticks to junior high ministry." The professor was unaware that Palmer was at the time pastor of the prestigious First Presbyterian Church in Berkeley, California.

So, is Earl Palmer a theologian or a teacher of junior high kids? By his own admission, he's both.

"I've never been anything but a Young Life leader," he once said, meaning that he's always been enthusiastic, passionate, and relevant in his preaching and teaching. In short, Palmer is a riveting communicator who knows how to integrate theology and life.

Palmer is now senior pastor of University Presbyterian Church in Seattle, Washington. Before that he was pastor of First Presbyterian Church, Berkeley, California. He has written a number of books and Bible commentaries, his latest releases being *Signposts: Living with Christian Values in an Age of Uncertainty* (Word) and *Integrity in a World of Pretense* (InterVarsity).

We eventually found the colored chalk in the supply room and even came up with some great craft ideas for first and second graders. And, as I later discovered, teachers did appreciate the larger perspective I gave to their teaching. And that is what teaching is about: attending to details *and* giving people a greater perspective.

That's exactly what our three authors do for us here. They discuss the trouble spots of teaching while enlarging our vision of the teaching task. In that way, they help us as we move, with them, on our way toward mastering teaching.

— *Mark Galli*
associate editor, LEADERSHIP
Carol Stream, Illinois

PART ONE

The Teacher's Task

Secular education seeks to make better, more effective, more successful, more intelligent people. The Christian educator aspires to nothing less than the transformation of a believer into the image of Christ.

— Howard Hendricks

CHAPTER ONE

What Makes Christian Education Distinct

As a teenager I was offered a scholarship to Northwestern University as a premed student. I am fascinated by the human body and love to watch surgery. But one year before going there the Lord impressed upon me: I could work on the body, which ultimately would deteriorate and die, or I could work on the soul, which will last forever.

I chose to be a physician of the soul. I gave up the scholarship and went to Wheaton College to prepare for ministry. It was one of the best decisions I have ever made, for I've become convinced that

Christian education, my field of ministry, is one of the highest of all callings.

I've also become convinced that pastors and Christian educators need to keep reminding themselves of the unique role of Christian education.

All around us we see status given to secular education. Children spend the bulk of their childhood in it. School board elections can become the focus of the entire community. Universities are the center of society's greatest research and most profound discoveries. The media constantly seek the opinions of university professors.

Amid all that, pastors and Christian educators are likely to feel like second-class educators, people who "merely" teach the Christian faith, while "real" educators are out there shaping the world.

Nothing could be further from the truth. So periodically, I like to remind myself and other Christian educators and pastors about the difference between secular education and our calling. Ultimately, I believe it's like the difference between being a physician of the body or a physician of the soul.

A Higher Perspective

In Christian education we deal with the transcendent. Secular education deals only with the human. Christian education discusses the eternal, secular education the here and now. In particular, there are four areas where this is evident.

• *A means of revelation.* Reason, the main staple of secular education, can go a long way, even in a Christian setting. It can assimilate and integrate and see the implications of what God reveals. But in our night drive into understanding, revelation is the headlights and reason the wheels; revelation helps us see the way that reason must follow.

Without revelation, in fact, the most important things in life are missed: without revelation, you cannot reason your way to the resurrection. Without revelation you cannot reason your way to the Trinity. Without revelation, you cannot reason your way to sacrificial love.

So, the Christian educator, being an instrument of revelation, is privileged to witness some remarkable moments.

As a hobby, I observe operations. Once a surgeon friend invited me to watch a stapedectomy, a microsurgical procedure on the three small bones of the inner ear, enabling a deaf person to hear. Since the surgery is not painful, the patient needs only a local anesthetic.

At one point in the operation, my friend said, "Howie, I'm going to join these bones now. As I do, I'll keep talking, and you watch this guy's face." The moment he connected those tiny bones, the patient's eyes opened wide. Tears of joy started pouring down his cheeks, and I wiped them with gauze.

That's what revelation is like. As I talk, the Holy Spirit joins the bones, imparts the insight. And when it happens, I can see it on my hearers' faces. Their eyes open; their minds are animated. Their lives are changed.

• *Concerned first with God.* Secular education assumes that human observations and interpretations are the basis of reality. Christian education assumes that since God is the Creator and Sovereign of all, he alone is the interpreter of all. All things serve him and are sustained by him. He guides history. Thus the very foundation of knowledge is different for the Christian educator.

The effect is dramatic, as telling as the difference between astronomy studied from a sun-centered versus earth-centered theory of the solar system. God-centered education puts all history into the right perspective; it brings meaning to literature, respect and sanctity to life, standards and authority to decisions about social problems, and direction to philosophy.

• *Concerned with things that last.* Christian education has the authority to speak about more than this visible world, the world that is passing away. Secular education can focus on business and money, matter and molecules, people and issues, but the Christian educator can move beyond to the soul, the human spirit, life after death, the kingdom of God, the return of Christ, the final judgment — things that last.

To put it another way, the difference between secular and Christian education is as stark as the difference between the animal and human world.

Animals and humans both have hearts, blood, and brains. They both live and die. They both reproduce sexually. They eat and breathe in remarkably similar ways. In the end, however, the differences infinitely exceed the likenesses. Only humans are created in the image of God. Only humans can make moral decisions. Only humans can perform surgery, rocket to the moon, write *Romeo and Juliet*, paint the Mona Lisa, build the Notre Dame Cathedral. And only humans will be resurrected in the image of Jesus Christ.

And only Christian education will impart to people the grandest and most vital truths of life.

● *Superintended by the Holy Spirit.* In Christian education the Holy Spirit is ultimately orchestrating the learning experience, in which I am but a participant. He, not me, oversees the classroom. He is the master teacher, not me. He is the medium of communication, the giver and transmitter of truth, and I am the personality he is animating.

The presence of the Holy Spirit requires the Christian educator to have an attitude of dependence and humility. I can draw back, beginning to depend on myself, my books, my experience, my past learning, my lesson plans, my messages. Or I can be sensitive to him, seek him, acknowledge daily in prayer that I can do nothing on my own, only what he does through me by his grace.

So, no matter what my scholastic degrees or expertise, I know that without total dependence on the Spirit, I cannot bear fruit; I cannot achieve my goal of full discipleship. I can transmit information without the Holy Spirit. I can explain and illustrate and entertain, but I cannot bear fruit without abiding in the vine.

Not Just to Teach But to Transform

Not only the perspective but the objective of Christian teaching transcends secular education. The secularist seeks to make better, more effective, successful, and intelligent people. The Christian educator aspires to nothing less than to transform people into the image of Christ.

Secular education and Christian education thus have different postures toward the world. One helps a person fit into the world system; the other helps lift a person above the world. I am teaching not merely to inform the mind but to renew the mind: "Do not conform any longer to the pattern of this world, but be transformed by the renewing of your mind. Then you will be able to test and approve what God's will is — his good, pleasing and perfect will" (Rom. 12:2).

I once took a graduate course at New York University. I knew the professor was brilliant, in complete command of his field. So on the first day of class, I sat in the front row; I didn't want to miss anything.

I soon noticed, however, that the other students crowded the back rows. These being graduate students, motivated learners, I couldn't understand it. But in a matter of minutes, I figured it out.

The professor was remote. He had little enthusiasm and simply droned on during the lecture. Later in the course he said to the class, "Look, I get paid whether you learn or not." Then I understood his cold approach to his subject.

As a Christian educator, that attitude will never do. My goal is not to lecture, or even to lecture with excellence. My goal is to teach in such a way that students both learn and employ their knowledge. Christian educators should view themselves as nothing less than disciplers. The knowledge we communicate affects more than the minds of our hearers; it should change lives.

In particular, I want to see my students develop five qualities as a result of my teaching.

Deepening Commitment to Christ

Secular education asks what students know, not who they are. Christian education asks not how much students know but how closely they are following Christ.

In Christian education what goes into the head must move to the heart, compelling deeper commitment and greater obedience. Spiritual knowledge is never intended for the head alone, never focused on skills alone, facts alone, principles alone. All knowledge must be dedicated to the glory of God.

While we may be tempted to assume that commitment is the hearer's responsibility alone, we know better. Teachers have a role to play, especially in calling people to obedience concerning what they have heard. I have found that I have a better chance of creating committed students when I challenge them with the implications of what they are learning, spelling out the application in specific terms.

Growing in Character

I want to see in my students the fruits of the Spirit. Mere knowledge is not my goal, but character.

Several years ago the headlines trumpeted the stories of a serial rapist in a town near Dallas. When the police finally nabbed the criminal, we got the bad news that he was an alumnus, a graduate of the seminary. He had studied, passed the tests, projected the image, gone off to pastor, but he had failed to develop character.

I can instruct in such a way that people are satisfied with listening while not doing. I can make them comfortable with increasing spiritual knowledge while they lack commitment and obedience. I can enable hearers to be puffed up with knowledge rather than humbled by their disobedience to that knowledge. If hearts are not being renewed along with minds, I have failed.

Showing Competence to Live Out the Faith

I am dedicated to giving my hearers the skills, knowledge, experience, and character necessary to bear fruit for Christ.

In the war against Iraq, the military stressed in briefings and interviews the professionalism of the modern American soldier. "The soldiers did their job like professionals," they would say. "We have trained them to be the best in the world." Military professionalism is valued for good reason: commanders know that a soldier's survival, as well as that of his unit, depends on his level of competence.

I feel the same way about equipping believers as a sergeant must feel in boot camp. I know that no Christian can become capable and qualified for the Lord's service without being taught certain skills. I don't want anyone to finish my class and be incapable of accomplishing God's purposes.

I think a Christian must be competent in three areas:

● *Knowledge.* Paul admitted that he lacked rhetorical skills and personal presence to impress the Corinthians, but he stressed that he did have truth, crucial knowledge that was far more important.

A student without a grasp of the Bible is a warrior without weapons. I am a teacher because I'm convinced knowledge makes a difference, especially in how believers live and how well they help others.

I was visiting a man in his home when he said, "You've got to watch this show." So I joined him and his wife and kids and watched TV. Among other things, the program treated immoral behavior lightly, as if it were something to joke about.

After it ended, he said, "Wasn't that great?"

I replied, "What messages do you think your kids are getting from this kind of stuff?"

Knowledge is more than the accumulation of facts. It includes the intellectual ability to critique contemporary books, song lyrics, and movies. So when discussing a modern book or movie, I regularly ask my students, "What are the values of the piece? What are the presuppositions? What is the scriptural perspective on this? What difference would it make if we acted on this way of looking at the world? How can we counteract the negatives?"

I am committed to training people who can learn for themselves, who do their own decision making, their own problem solving, their own creative thinking, their own biblical interpretation. I want them to learn not only what, not only why, but how.

● *Emotions.* True knowledge prompts feelings. Several years ago I flew to Africa to see Byang Katto, a key leader of the African Evangelical Fellowship. I took in the sights and sounds and smells of mission life in Nigeria.

When we drove in the back country of Nigeria, I have never felt so close to death — people drive like crazed race drivers. And when vehicles break down, they just stop in the middle of the road.

You can be speeding over a hill and *whack* — it's all over before you see anything.

Well, when I returned to my room, Jeanne said, "Howie, what in the world is the matter?"

"Why?" I replied.

"You're white as a sheet," she said.

I described my ride and said, "Jeanne, we have to pray for these missionaries with a whole new emphasis! They face this kind of danger every day."

My personal knowledge of that missionary's experience improved my prayers for all missionaries. I now *feel* their challenges and dangers. Feelings aren't everything, but they are a vital part of a full apprehension of the truth.

If we're not careful, we can suck all the blood out of the heart with facts and information. Instead, I want to enlarge my hearers' hearts as much as I do their brains. I want them to know the truth and feel strongly about it.

● *Action.* A competent Christian acts out the faith. Jesus was powerful in word *and deed* — a man of action. So are his followers.

Some years ago I had a student who had been practicing law in Atlanta when he gave his life to Christ. He had come to the seminary to earn a theological degree, but when he completed his work he returned to the Southeast. Today he teaches and disciples young attorneys, representing Jesus Christ in the bar association. That's action.

Action, of course, fulfills and strengthens knowledge and feeling. Consequently, it's a mistake to delay ministering to others till "someday when I'm ready to serve the Lord."

So I arouse my students to ministry. I inquire personally about their spiritual gifts, whether they are using them and what obstacles they have come up against. Their particular ministry may have little to do with the subject I am teaching, but it directly affects how well they assimilate any knowledge. Ministry plugs knowledge into real people and their 110-volt problems.

Creative in Ministry

I don't want to produce cookie-cutter Christians, patterned after my image. Everyone has a unique personality, gifts, and calling; I want to teach each person to make the most of that uniqueness.

I want people to be resourceful at getting answers from the Word, to learn from their creative God, to find ways to minister to other's needs, to solve their own problems. I want them to find and apply principles, not formulas, in different settings and situations.

Grant, for example, left the seminary classroom to serve in the military chaplaincy. His desire to reach unchurched personnel led him to schedule Sunday evening meetings — at the same time first-run movies from Hollywood were usually shown on the base. Others said no one would come, but he imported films with a Christian message and followed the showings with discussion and a presentation of the gospel, laced with music and testimonies.

In just a few weeks the "Sunday Night Gospel Hour" attendance equaled the secular entertainment, and far exceeded the Sunday morning chapels. Grant was simply adapting his ministry to the setting.

I want people to learn and grow on their own, not to depend on my answers. That's tougher than it sounds, for the more insightful the teacher, the more dependent the hearers become. So I've had to check my impulse to impress people with my insights and instead challenge them to think. I spend a lot of time asking questions, letting students struggle, pointing them to the One who wants to help, letting students get into sink-or-swim situations. Need, I've noticed, is like flint: it sparks creativity.

Effective Communicators

Communication — receiving and giving information and understanding — is at the heart of our faith. We cannot grow in our relationship with God or reach out effectively to others unless we learn some fundamental communication skills. In particular, I want my students to gain proficiency in the two main areas of communication.

● *Listening.* Good communication begins with good listening. And good listening begins with hearing and understanding God's Word. We cannot hope to speak to basic human needs until we understand what they are and how to deal with them from God's perspective.

So, I am committed to training people to read and study the Scriptures for themselves. I do this not by repeatedly exhorting them to read the Word, or just holding them accountable for daily devotional reading, but by whetting their appetite for the Word.

I work hard to make the Bible relevant, alive, exciting. In addition, people will more readily read the Word when they have a frame of reference for understanding it, so I equip hearers with basic principles of interpretation and the big picture of Scripture.

With one young woman, when I simply placed the books of the Bible in chronological order, enabling her to see how each fit into God's overall plan, her eyes lit up.

"It's like the clouds are clearing out of my sky," she said. "I'm beginning to see God's purpose for people in the world — and for me!"

A Christian teacher trains disciples who listen intently to the Word of God but who also are aware and interested in others. They aren't just interested in expressing their own opinions. They are curious, hungry for knowledge, sensitive to what others think, retentive.

● *Speaking.* "Speaking" takes many forms, of course, one of which is writing. In order to help students learn to express their thoughts clearly and cogently, I urge them to record on paper their walk with the Lord, to write down spiritual goals, devotional thoughts, prayers, personal evaluations, and Bible studies. Such writing lays the ground work for any speaking they end up doing, whether formally or not.

I may not insist that all my students be able to speak in front of a group, but I do want them to be able to tell others why they believe in Christ, or in Peter's words, to give a ready answer for the hope that is in them.

Furthermore, I encourage students to verbalize their ideas,

either privately or with others. Students may think they know something after listening to me teach or after reading a book, but when they try to tell someone else what they know, they discover which areas of the subject they know little about. That encourages them to more thorough study. Also, the very process of telling can clarify what is foggy in the mind. We learn by speaking, just as we learn by writing.

Knowing the Greatest Joy

One day when my daughter was in high school, she said to me, "Daddy, I know you're busy, but you've got to come to our parent/teacher night. You have to meet my biology teacher."

The night of the event, we arrived late and sat in the back row. I heard a scratchy voice from the front, but I couldn't see the teacher. He was sitting down, describing all the experiments his students were doing, one incredible scientific project after another.

I finally stood to see better and discovered that the teacher was in a wheelchair, a polio victim. His presentation impressed me so much, I went up afterward to talk to him. I found out he had two Ph.D.'s and that several area universities had sought him as a professor.

"Why in the world do you keep teaching in high school?" I asked.

"Can you think of anything more exciting," he replied, "than molding young, plastic minds?"

He had the right attitude for teaching, and that was why my daughter and the other students responded so well to him.

The only thing I can imagine more exciting than molding plastic minds is the privilege of molding plastic lives and producing souls for eternity. And that, finally, is the unique role of Christian education.

Knowing what subject to teach and how to teach it can become less of a mystery and more of a ministry.
— Roberta Hestenes

CHAPTER TWO

Knowing What to Teach, and How

When I was on staff at Las Canada Presbyterian Church, a group of women said to me, "We want to do a small group Bible study, but we want more than a series of Bible lessons. Frankly, we get bored and turned off by that."

Since these women were from Hollywood, I agreed that they would need something a little more creative. So I began by asking what was going on in their lives, where they were struggling, how meaningful their prayer lives were, what they were learning about their faith.

From that I got a fix on their needs and their learning style. Together we designed a study on the Book of Psalms that became a turning point for many of the women.

Not only did they read and meditate on the Psalms, section by section, they also danced, sang, and wrote their own versions of them. They ended up doing a presentation of the Psalms for some other women in the church. They lived in the Psalms in a way that changed their lives.

Preparing to teach people — and not just a subject — is one of the most challenging aspects of the teaching ministry. Sometimes we hit it right on the mark, like the Psalms study. Sometimes one or more things don't click, and the class becomes increasingly sparse as the weeks pass, finally ending in a whimper — and this in spite of the fact we're teaching the most vital message known to humankind.

Sometimes the reason for the dismal class is obvious — lack of teacher preparation or competition from other classes offered during the same hour. Other times, we can't quite figure out what's going on.

That's a discouraging experience for class and teacher alike. But it can be avoided, or considerably lessened. I've taught on two church staffs and have taught education at seminars and seminary, and I've noticed over the years that if a few principles are followed, knowing what to teach and how to teach it becomes less of a mystery and more of a ministry.

Prerequisite Attitudes

Some college classes have prerequisites for students. In the church, I think there are prerequisites for teaching, not just the technical qualifications needed but the attitudes necessary. In particular, I find that I teach better when I keep three goals firmly fixed in my mind.

First, I want to take people seriously. I don't just want to entertain or impress people. This is not show-and-tell time. I want to choose and teach subjects that really matter to people with an eternal destiny.

I think it's terrible stewardship for a class on building Christian relationships to sit around answering the question, "What is your favorite vegetable?" People are dealing with life-and-death issues, and they don't need to sit around talking about their favorite vegetable. I think you can build nurturing relationships as you interact with significant content that challenges and deepens Christian understanding.

This doesn't mean everything has to be deep, somber, and serious. In fact, learning needs to be fun; it should intrigue. But whatever we do needs to be worthy of people's time.

Second, I want people to learn and grow as Christians. My goal isn't to display my learning, to teach creatively, to convey information, or a host of other things. Instead, I want most of all to see changed lives — obedient Christian disciples in the world.

Many years ago, while teaching a series on Romans, a member of the class said to me, "I love your teaching on Romans. You make it so clear. I really feel like I understand it when I'm with you. I feel dumb when I read it myself at home; I can't make any sense out of it."

She thought she was complimenting me. It was actually a rebuke. She was impressed that *I* understood Romans. But she didn't. She couldn't read her Bible for herself and make sense out of it.

But I'm not going to be with her when she hits a crisis and needs to know that Romans 8 is God's Word to her, or when she's struggling with the messed up social order and needs to make sense out of the environment and how a Christian deals with that.

So, when I'm done with a class, I measure my effectiveness as a teacher by answering the question "Have these people learned a little better how to be disciples of Jesus Christ?"

Third, I want people to experience authentic Christian community. Jesus may call us as individuals but only so that we might join others in the journey of faith. Discipleship is communal, not isolated. We not only need to love one another, we really need each other in order to live the Christian life. It's crucial in my teaching that I help people connect with each other, like the group of women did who studied the Psalms.

After I started keeping these goals in mind, the way I prepared and taught were dramatically transformed. In fact, the rest of the principles I share are built on this tripod foundation. Getting to know the people I'm going to teach is a critical part of this process. But once that is in order, other matters must be attended to as well.

Know, Feel, Do

When I teach a class, I want to affect the whole person, not just the mind but also the heart, and not just the heart and mind but also the will. So as I prepare, I ask myself three questions.

1. What do I want them to know? It never hurts to remind myself of some of the fundamentals of learning, for instance, that we must learn at foundational levels before we can learn at higher levels. We need knowledge before we can apply it; we need to dissect material before we can put it together in a new way.

Too often, in our hurry to get to application, we design courses that assume knowledge that our people don't have. The result is that people are given more than they can handle, and learning doesn't occur. We can also fail if we underestimate what people know.

I know one pastor who taught a class in Galatians, hoping to introduce the class to Paul. By the time the class was over, he realized he had failed to capitalize on his people's knowledge: they already knew Paul; they were ready to grapple with the deeper texture of the book. He had misread the knowledge his people had.

I also have to make sure that I teach what people need to know, not just what I find interesting. For example, one fifty-year-old man in a new members class I was teaching told me he didn't know any other prayer except the one his mother taught him as a child: "Now I lay me down to sleep . . ." He was embarrassed, but he didn't know anything else.

Since there were others like him in the class, I had to resist my urge to talk about prayer at a deeper level. Instead I focused on the fundamentals, answering questions like: What kinds of prayer are there? What is intercession? How do you do it? How do you carve out ten minutes a day? What do you say when you pray? What does the Lord's Prayer mean? What are some patterns of prayer that work for people in the midst of busy lives? How do you pray when you're in the car all day?

So I can't start teaching until I'm clear about what my people need to know.

2. What do I want them to feel? Learning is more than assimilating and applying knowledge. I'm teaching people, after all, not programming computers. So I also want to design the class so that it makes a difference in how people feel. This happens in two ways.

First, depending on the topic of the class, I want the class to feel the emotion the Scripture text conveys. If we're studying a Psalm of lament, I want them during the class to feel some of that lament. If the passage is about praise, I want them to feel like praising God by the end. If I'm talking about Christian community, I want them to experience at least a little of that by the end of the course. At the most basic level, I want them to "enjoy" God.

Second, I want people to enjoy the learning experience so that they will continue to want to learn. If people feel attracted to the subject even after the class, pursuing it on their own through reading or research, I know I've done my job. If they finish the class with a sigh of relief, "I'm glad I'm done with that. I will never study that again!" then I've not engaged their emotions effectively.

3. What do I want them to do? I'm concerned about what people do in the class and outside it.

In a class on the spiritual disciplines, for instance, I will not only want people to know what the disciplines are and to be intrigued about practicing them; I also want to help them begin doing them. Knowing that accountability helps with action, I might have individuals pick partners from the class to discuss week by week how they are doing with their Bible reading or prayer.

Whatever the course subject, I want them to practice what Paul in Romans calls "the obedience of faith." I want them to love and obey God more faithfully.

Let the Text Shape the Class

Naturally, the subject will determine how I design a class, but it does that in more ways than one. This is especially true when I'm teaching a class on some book of the Bible.

For example, if I'm going to teach Ephesians 4 through 6, which is about building community, I need to do more than talk about building community. We must experience community in the class in some way. At minimum, that would mean group discussion of the text. It might mean breaking the class into twos or fours or helping people find class prayer partners.

It's not only vital to teach *what* the text teaches but also, if possible, *how* it teaches it. I'm interested both in the message and in the way the message is communicated. That will be different in the prophets than in Revelation than in the Psalms — very different!

And then within books, different passages will require a different approach. Within the Psalms alone, for instance, we have joy, lament, contrition, despair, and thankfulness. If we're going to be studying a Psalm of contrition, then, part of the learning may involve experiencing pain — maybe I'll ask the class to spend a few moments recalling privately some sin that has burdened them and then leading a silent time of confession.

Approaching the text in this way means I don't have to tie up every lesson in a little package and put a bow on it and say, "Now, go out and do X, Y, and Z." Not every passage is so neatly tied, nor does every passage of the Bible have a direct application.

What can you say after studying Romans 1:18-32? Don't sin? That's pretty obvious. Thank God for God's grace? Certainly, but at that point in Romans, there's nothing suggested about what we're supposed to do. Paul will get to that, and when he does, so will I.

In the end, it's a matter of trusting Scripture for both the message and the medium of the message.

Blocking the Class

Once I see what I want people to know, feel, and do, I'm ready to block the class: I determine what my time frame is — six weeks, ten weeks, a whole year — and then decide when and how I will mix knowing, feeling, and doing in the class.

For example, if I've got thirteen weeks to teach Romans — a sixteen-chapter book, and a "thick" book at that — I have to figure out when I will slow down and when I will summarize. How will I divide the subject week by week into the time available?

Let's also say that I've decided to address the Jewish-Christian questions raised in chapters 9 through 11. Maybe I think the people I'm teaching have some unhealthy attitudes towards Jews, so I'll want to spend three weeks on this section.

The first week I may simply spend the hour getting people to see the theology of those chapters. The next week we may discuss some contemporary Jewish-Christian issues (Jewish evangelism, the Middle East political situation). The week after that, I may want to help the class experience the sense of awe that Paul felt over God's sovereign dealings with the Jews. With that priority in mind, I will see that I can only cover chapters 1 through 3 in summary fashion, 4–8 more slowly, and 12–16 more quickly.

On the other hand, if I have thirteen weeks to cover the six chapters of Galatians, I may want to block the book so I can spend a whole lesson on a couple of verses in chapter 6, focusing on "Bear one another's burdens and so fulfill the law of Christ." If I've blocked the book, identifying my priorities for the subject matter, I won't feel I'm spinning my wheels by spending so much time on relatively little material.

When I block the course, I highlight the concerns I've determined need addressing. I'm no longer subject to plodding along, trying to cover material in equal chunks, using the same format week after week.

Choosing a Teaching Method

Teachers have a number of tools in the teaching tool chest. Effective planning involves choosing the right tool for the right job.

• *Lecture.* Lecture is a good way to cover large amounts of material (e.g., the major views of the Book of Revelation) or complex issues (e.g., the relationship between New Age teaching and orthodox theology). On the down side, lecture does not demand much of students and so can make them passive.

Still lecturing can be one of the best ways to convey information, especially if information is put together in a way not done before. If someone has put the material I want to cover in a book chapter or article, then I simply get permission to copy and pass out that material. That's a better use of class time. Instead, if I lecture, I want to integrate themes and topics in a fresh way.

● *Individual study and reflection.* This can also be a powerful way to handle content, especially if you give people guidance during their study. One pastor I know often begins his Bible studies by asking people to reflect silently on the passage for ten minutes, giving them two or three questions to guide their thinking. Sometimes written outlines can help people stay focused during the time of reflection.

This does a couple of things. First, it shows people that with a little perseverance, they can study the Bible by themselves. Sometimes this guided reflection is the only time people discipline themselves to study the Bible alone.

Second, this "primes the pump" for the discussion that follows. People discover themes and questions in the text that are important to them, things a mini-lecture on the teacher's part would miss. People are forced to engage the text, but before long it engages them.

● *Group investigation.* This is a way you can make use of material already put together well by others. If I've found a great journal article or a Bible dictionary article, I'll put people into groups and have them read the material. I'll also give them a question (e.g., "What is the definition of *grace* according to this author?" or "What are the principle ways people deal with personal trauma according to the article?" This not only is a way to deliver content, it also starts building relationships.

● *Group discussion.* Group discussion can occur only after people have been provided with information, either from lecture or group investigation, for instance. In group discussion they respond and work with the information they have.

For example, after discussing the background and interpretation of 1 Corinthians 14, on the role of women in the church, I might have them discuss their reactions to a newspaper clipping about a conservative denomination excommunicating a church for calling a woman as senior pastor.

Naturally, group discussion and group investigation are the heart of most small group Bible studies, where the Bible itself is the "article" under discussion.

● *Breaking into twos or fours.* This is a variation on group discussion. I've used this in small groups and when I've spoken to a thousand people. I ask people to turn to the person next to them and talk for three to five minutes about something I've just taught, say, the problem of evil in Job. The question might be *when, if ever have you felt closest to Job?*

It not only wakes people from lecture slumber, it connects them to another person. Also it requires no trained leadership, whereas breaking up into groups of six or more usually does. Finally, I've found few people who are offended by being asked to talk with just one other person if the question is not too personal.

What Makes for a Good Question?

As you can see, most of my methods rely on getting people to talk to one another. And that requires that I ask them questions that will elicit fruitful discussion. As I prepare my class, then, I carefully craft my questions, remembering these characteristics of a good question:

● *It can be answered by the people asked.* That means I have to ask questions about things people know. They know, for instance, about their own experience. So, "When did you first realize that grace was more than just a word?" is more likely to work than "What are the three principle views of the atonement?" I can ask the latter question only when I've given them, through lecture or group investigation, information upon which to base their answer.

It also means I must take into account the unique experiences of people in the class. In a class of men and women, many women will be left out of a question like "When did you get your first car?"

- *It is interesting to everyone in the room.* Some questions fall flat because they ask for information simplistically ("In John 3:16, how do we know God loved the world?") or abstractly ("What does it mean to love?"). An interesting question will touch on a specific concern of most of the people present.

Recently, I gave a seminar on women in leadership. I knew the women attending were vitally interested in the topic, so a simple question like "Where do you think women most struggle in balancing their multiple roles today?" grabbed their attention.

Some questions, of course, merely set up other questions, so they won't be interesting in themselves. "What are the three principle views of the atonement?" is not inherently interesting, unless it leads immediately to something like, "What theory do you feel is the most faithful to the biblical text?"

- *It is clear and simple.* If you have to define words or phrases in the question, it's probably not a good one. "In light of John's eschatology, his view of last things, what would you say is the call of Christians today — what is the thing Christians are to do?" can be clarified considerably: "If according to John, good will win out, what difference can that make in our lives?"

- *It requires a thoughtful response.* The question should not have an obvious answer. That not only bores people, it wastes class time. Better to simply state the answer in a declarative sentence and get to the meaty question: not "How does God show his love to the world in John 3:16?" but "God shows love by giving what is precious to him. What precious thing are you being called to give this week as an act of love?"

Again, a set-up question may be used quickly, but the following question must demand something of the class. People should have to draw on their experience or put together diverse themes or integrate the teaching into their lives. Consequently, questions with yes or no or multiple choice answers are rarely helpful.

- *It will protect people's dignity.* A good question doesn't separate people based on their knowledge, as in "Where else in the Bible do we find a discussion of the relationship between husbands and wives?" Right away, Bible novices in the class feel intimidated.

Also, a good question will not embarrass people. Naturally, if I want people to share personally, I may need to ask some questions that will risk that. But if I know my group, I'll have a sense about the limits of a personal question.

For example, when I've studied 2 Corinthians 8, about giving, I've asked, "How nervous do you get when you talk with other people about the way you spend money?" It helps people be a little transparent without asking them to reveal too much.

As you can see, preparing questions is not something that can be done on the spur of the moment. They make or break most classes I teach, so I give a good deal of attention to crafting them.

Working Together

I once taught a class on the Book of Revelation, and one part of the class became a task force, which was assigned the challenge of finding art and music that had been based on the Book of Revelation.

By the end of the class, they had gathered enough material to lead the last session. They presented slides showing the great works of Western art and played music of great composers, like Handel, displaying for ear and eye how the new heaven and new earth has been interpreted. It was a magnificent conclusion to the class.

But even more magnificent was what happened to the people, especially those in that task force. They met regularly throughout the course. They dug deep into Revelation, thought hard about John's imagery, and found resources to help them understand John.

They also found one another. They didn't have a relationship before the class started. They were just people who happened to share an interest in the last book of the Bible. By the end of the course they were good friends in Christ.

That to me was the epitome of what teaching is about: getting people immersed in the Word and in touch with one another. When I've helped people do that, I know I've prepared well.

I avoid Sunday morning meanderings by cultivating textual fluency, people fluency, and schedule fluency.
— *Earl Palmer*

CHAPTER THREE

Preparing Yourself to Teach

N o one wants to blur or block the message of the Lord. Yet, sometimes on Sunday morning we climb into the pulpit or stand behind a lectern and, for any host of reasons, haltingly deliver an ill-prepared message or lead a Bible study that just goes nowhere.

The symptoms of such sermons and classes vary: (a) use of cliches, due to a shallow grasp of the text, (b) fogginess, due to heavy biblical spade work but light cultivation for human consumption, (c) apathy, due to sparse focus on the implications of the text. But whatever the symptoms, the source is often the same: lack of preparedness.

These defects can be corrected. In particular, I avoid Sunday morning meanderings by cultivating three fluencies during the week: textual fluency, people fluency, and schedule fluency. Let me illustrate this by showing how I prepare for preaching, which for me is the main format for my teaching.

Textual Fluency

Textual fluency means knowing the content of a Scripture passage thoroughly enough that it leaves its mark on me. And textual fluency requires a journey from biblical text understood to discipleship implication addressed. In my journey, I take five steps, posing five questions to every preaching passage.

First, there are the technical questions, such as vocabulary study. C. S. Lewis says, "Tell me what the hard words mean" (in their own setting, when they were first said). He maintained that a lexicon profited him more than a thousand commentaries. After all, a text is built with words.

Second comes historical work. I must view the text in its own setting, both the historical within the material itself and that which lies behind the material. The historical research within would be, for instance, to learn about the identity of a person mentioned. Who is John the Baptist? Who are the Pharisees? Or the Sadducees?

To discover the historical question behind the material I need to figure out, for example, what issue caused Paul to write what he did to Timothy. Or in the case of John 1, I might ask, *Why would John interrupt his opening prologue three times to explain that John the Baptist is not the Messiah? Was the identity of John the Baptist a hot issue?*

The third question is theological: If that's what it says, what does it mean? This requires some interpretation, which is the dynamic part of the great journey.

For example, when I determine that the parable of the Prodigal Son is not about the son as much as the father, that's a theological evaluation. I'm saying, "Here's what he's getting at." Of course, I should be a modest learner and compare what theologians and commentators through the ages have said about a text, as a check against my biases.

The fourth step is the contemporary question. I ask, "Now, how would Christ's point collide with his own world, with his contemporaries?" In the parable of the Prodigal Son we see within the text itself a collision occurring between Jesus and the Pharisees over his eating and drinking with publicans.

At that point, I play a game with the text and ask, *I wonder how the Pharisees would respond? Who would they identify with? How would they feel about what Jesus does with the elder son?* Now I'm getting inside the skin of a first-century person — what some critics call audience criticism — to understand how and why the collision would occur.

By the way, the better ancient historian I am, the better I can do that. The more I know about Paul's contemporary Nero, and the historical situation during his reign as emperor, the better I can understand Paul's allusions to Rome in Philippians. The more I know about ancient Jewish culture, the better I can understand references to the Pharisees. That's where research pays rich dividends.

The final step is the discipleship question, where I put myself personally and representatively under the text. I must ask, "What is this text saying to me? How does it collide with my life? Where am I challenged to change?"

That's the study journey I take in preparing for preaching and teaching. Obviously the journey demands time and work, both of which I gladly invest in order to avoid three dangers:

● *Inaccuracy.* Research prevents historical errors, which can cripple the message. If I say something inaccurate in an illustration about airplanes, the pilots and aircraft-hobbyists in the congregation will downgrade everything else I say.

When it comes to biblical material, I must be accurate also because (1) the Scriptures deserve it, and (2) the people, whom I am beckoning to journey with me, deserve it. So I respect them by being accurate, fulfilling my professional promise, like the doctor who promises not to get sloppy with drug prescriptions.

● *Flatness.* Research kindles a valid urgency. After significant study the material itself grips you.

One education study of a few years ago sought to discover the factors that raise teenagers' SAT scores. They found one particular variable that did that: teachers who believed their subject matter was crucial, who felt a student couldn't make it without knowing their subject. Instructors who know the material but couldn't care less if you learn it, or strict disciplinarians who merely want the right paper at the right time but don't seek true learning, are less effective. I must passionately believe the scriptural material is invaluable. That comes, in my experience, from seeing the gospel collide first with the first-century world, then with twentieth-century world views, and watching it hold true through time.

● *Limiting the gospel.* We don't want to shortcut the journey by prematurely deciding what discipleship implications we want to affirm. For example, a well-meaning pastor may say, "I want to tell people God loves them," and then simply hunt for some supporting verses on Saturday night to undergird his or her intuitions. But often the verses don't. Nevertheless, they wedge the verses into the message.

This approach doesn't give the full gospel a chance to break through. But if I can help listeners discover the text for themselves, then they will see what the text actually says. They can go even further than me, then, moving in directions unforeseen by me, because they are able to explore the text, not just my theology. This can happen when I am textually fluent.

People Fluency

Some pastors love working the early stages of the journey but never get around to asking what it all means. They can stun us with Greek word studies but never arrive at discipleship implications.

Truth be known, we may be wanting to hide in the text, always talking about what the text says; as long as I don't get down to what it means, it never really bothers me or anyone else. Then I'm not meddling. There is a comfortable distance in "On the one hand Calvin said this. On the other, Luther said that. Bultmann went this way, and Barth that way." But what about me and you? What are we going to do?

That's where people fluency — understanding myself and my people — comes in. By sustained listening, I understand the questions on their minds, where they're coming from and what's happening in their lives. In fact, I can be a prophetic speaker to them only when I've been a prophetic listener.

For example, when I'm with teenagers, I try to understand what motivates and energizes their culture. Since it's sometimes strange to me, I'm tempted to distance or disconnect myself from it, or, what's worse, disdain or criticize it too quickly. Instead, I try to shift into a learner mode. When teenagers are bragging about some new music, I ask myself, *What is it that really turns them on about that music? What do they feel when they hear it? What do they like about that group?*

A prophetic listener is quick to hear and slow to speak. You can attend an opera, for instance, in the closed mode saying to yourself, *This is going to be boring,* or in the learner mode, *I wonder what has caused the Italians to love these operas so much?* A prophetic listener pauses to listen and watch.

I practice this skill in many settings. In train stations and airports, I watch people, observing what they're reading and listening closely to what they're saying. While attending a film that people are raving about, I try to figure out why they think it's so important. What value system is gripping them?

When I have a great text to communicate and I'm trying to find a window for my listeners, it's essential to know the questions they're asking and how they're asking them. Really there are no new questions, just ancient questions asked in new ways. So I've got to listen for how they're being asked, so that I can pose questions to the text on behalf of my people.

Schedule Fluency

I want to explode one myth. I believe pastors have the gift of time more than most professionals. Except for Sunday morning, pastors wield the whip hand over most events in the church week. We largely control when people will schedule appointments with us, when special classes will be offered, when we'll talk with outsiders. Granted, this scarcely means we abound in free time, but given our authority, we can, if the resolve is there, establish a rhythm to our week.

I have found that in order to be a good student (and for the sake of my sanity) every day needs to be different. I ease up at one point while toiling at another, interact with people at one point and withdraw at another. With such a rhythm I can reserve study time. But when every day is a jumble of random sameness, I'll never stay balanced; these are the kinds of days that create burnout.

The key for me is to see my life in units of seven days. Rarely can I spin one day in balance, and I can't think in terms of a year or even a month; that's too long. But seven days — that biblical model works for me: Six days shalt thou labor, one day shalt thou rest.

Monday I meet with church committees, write my newsletter columns, pen correspondence, meet with individuals. Tuesday I'm with my staff. Wednesday I have classes and my prayer group and teach an adult class across town.

Thursday morning I finish my sermon for the coming Sunday. I can do that because Thursday afternoon and Friday is uncontaminated time (with Saturday as my day off). On the previous Thursday afternoon I have excavated for this next week's sermon, and on Friday I've done general research.

Advancing deadlines for essentials, like the sermon, has helped me escape the garbled tyranny of the urgent. When pastors wait until Saturday to pound out their sermons, the undone sermon has overshadowed every day of that week. This kills thorough research. Therefore I begin preparing Sunday's sermon a week and a half early, and finish it the week it's due by Thursday noon.

This helps me use Friday in freedom. Friday I can read *Les Miserables* or the latest book on C. S. Lewis or a new commentary on John. I couldn't do this if my unfinished sermon was hanging over my head.

In addition, this allows me to know what I'm going to say a week in advance. I always preach and teach better today when I know that. The kitchen sink doesn't get thrown in every sermon.

So after mortaring the capstone into this Sunday's sermon text, I begin immediately on next week's, allowing me to enter the pulpit on Sunday knowing virtually everything I'm going to say the following week. That gives me tremendous freedom.

My week becomes a rhythm, then, a rhythm that enables me to become textual and people fluent.

Paying the Rent to Become Fluent

I never ask if I can do research. Does a doctor ask a patient, "Would you mind if I consult books?" Rather, I regard research as *sine qua non*. Gordon Fee, the New Testament scholar, once said to a group of us at a pastor's conference, "We've got the best story to tell; we must believe this in our bones and know, therefore, that it deserves thoroughgoing study."

Nevertheless, we cannot achieve schedule fluency — and therefore textual and people fluency — without cooperation from the congregation. Yet I've found that people will grant freedom for whatever we hold to be the linchpins in our ministry, especially if we're careful to "pay the rent."

To do anything valid in a church, anything we crave in ministry, we must earn the right. A tenant pays the rent before enjoying a house; otherwise he's continually looking over his shoulder for the landlord. After paying the rent, he relaxes. He can do most anything he wants there. In the same way a pastor pays at least four rents for the freedom to pursue the essentials of his ministry.

● *People must perceive that we know and are under the text.* A physician won't be allowed to treat a patient's ills unless the patient is confident the physician knows the medicines being prescribed. Otherwise the patient will be jumpy, watching the doctor's every move, worrying about the accuracy of everything he says.

Pastors must master the Scriptures and proclaim them clearly. In addition, our lives are to be under the Word, congruent with it. In his letters to the Ephesians and Philippians Paul says, "I want your life to be worthy of the gospel." The Greek word for *worthy* also means "congruent." We don't have to be perfect, but people must feel that our life affirms the message.

● *People must sense growth in us.* If not, they worry about us and, ironically, give us less time to study. They begin to hover around us, discipling us because they think we're going stale, going downhill. They expect a payoff for what they're allowing. Seeing growth, they want us to do even more of whatever caused it. They'll say, "Hey, listen, whatever you're doing, keep doing it."

● *People must know we're working hard.* We don't have to publish a work schedule, because most of the time people can catch it, feel it, when we're working hard. By our actions and demeanor they sense vigor. They sense an honest day's work for an honest day's wage. It's not the pastor waving his flag and saying, "I work so hard." (Besides, people often pinch the freedoms of a workaholic.) They just sense the pastor's pulling his oar.

● *People must know we love them.* When pastors show that they like their people and treasure them, the people go to bat for the pastor. If they are convinced the pastor is for them, they'll let the pastor take the time to become text and people fluent.

For me there is no substitute for learning the names of people and giving people my full attention when I'm with them. I can't be everywhere at every time I'm needed. But when I am with people, I must really *be there.* The church is real people in a real place, and the pastor must be a real person in that place.

Preteens and teenagers especially appreciate that non-exploitive adult who is simply friendly. It isn't necessary to have a profound word to say, but it is important to use their names and work at knowing them individually.

I once read an article in *The New York Times* by Norman Mailer on the subject of writing. He observed that some of his best writing had been done at times when, ironically, he was the driest. That's because when dry, he did more research, which resulted in some of his best breakthroughs.

At any given moment, sweet fluency, whether with people, text, or schedule, can seem like an unreachable goal. And that's just the time to give ourselves wholeheartedly to becoming fluent. For that's just when we may be closer to eloquence and effectiveness than we think.

Part Two

Challenges of
Church Education

Every class is diverse. I will never know all the mysteries of people's souls. But by God's grace, I can effectively address that diversity.

— *Roberta Hestenes*

CHAPTER FOUR
Not Everyone Learns Alike

J ohn lays floor tiles for a living, eight hours a day, day in and day out. He's not much of a reader, but he's eager to learn, and he's looking for something from the class I'm about to teach.

Peter is a lawyer, driven, compulsive, and a bit of a snob. He is a reader, and a skeptical one at that. In fact, he's vowed that if this class doesn't grab him, he probably won't bother with another.

Joanne's husband left her a few months ago, and now she's trying to support herself and her two children on a clerk's salary at Penney's. This is the first job she has had in twenty-five years. She doesn't think she's capable of anything better, and she feels absolutely powerless.

Michael owns his own small corporation; he's pretty much in charge of his time. He talks flippantly about time pressures and taxes, but he knows he's got it good. But he's feeling a vague sense of guilt about what to do with himself outside of his job.

These people and more sit before me as I'm about to begin a church school class. Only some vague attraction to the topic, a Bible study on Romans, binds them together. For a brief moment, I despair: *Each of these people comes with unique concerns and unique situations. How can I possibly communicate with all of them?*

This great diversity is one of the most humbling realities for the teacher. So over the years, I've learned to depend increasingly on the Holy Spirit to touch the diverse lives of my students. I've also learned that by God's grace some teaching techniques can address that diversity.

Variety in the classroom is of two types, and we must concern ourselves with both. First, people learn in a variety of ways: some absorb a lecture, others can't remember a thing until they've talked about it; some are readers, others are not. Some are creative and learn by using their imagination, by seeing images; others require the security of rote learning.

Second, people have a variety of emotional and spiritual concerns as they enter a classroom. Some are actively seeking Christ; others take him for granted; others still are on the verge of checking out of Christianity.

Let me begin by showing how I deal with the variety of emotional and spiritual interests present in a class.

Putting Needs into Perspective

Before I become overwhelmed with the variety of needs present in a class, I try to put people's concerns into perspective. That happens especially as I pray and reflect on these truths:

• *Only God knows people's real needs.* Only God knows where people are. Only God can judge the heart. This means two things.

First, I can draw on God to give me sensitivity to the real needs of people. That means I must pray for the members of my class. Praying for my class, person by person, not only lifts them to God, it sensitizes me to their situations. It helps me "see" them, so that they are registered in my mind as real persons. I'm not teaching a class as much as I'm teaching Hal and Susan and Joan and Bryan.

Second, as I immerse myself in prayer, I begin to trust God to work despite my ignorance of the private needs of people. I don't have to work myself into a frenzy trying to figure out all the needs present. Naturally, I must learn as much as I can in conversation, interviews, and the like. But ultimately I have to recognize that I can't possibly know everything necessary about people.

In fact, God often guides my thinking and planning so I end up meeting needs I'm not even aware of. All teachers have had people come up to them after class saying, "How did you know? That was just for me." That happens more often when I've spent sufficient time in prayer before preparing a class.

● *Someone is looking for God.* Over the years I've learned that no matter how blasé or how committed the class looks, someone there is in the midst of making a major decision about God.

In one Bible class I enjoyed the presence of a school teacher; she was one of the most active participants. Only in a personal conversation some months later did I discover that she didn't consider herself a Christian when she joined the class. She had never joined the church because she had never "gotten around to it," but the real reason was she did not feel she had a personal relationship with Christ. She had prayed for that a number of times, but "nothing had happened." She had sat through my class hoping that somehow God would touch her.

That insight led to a deeper conversation and reminded me that I must not take people's faith for granted.

● *Someone is about to give up on God.* The longer I've been teaching, the more I assume that life is beating hard on somebody in the room. Someone is concerned deeply about their marriage or a wayward child; perhaps someone has just lost a job. Whatever the cause, someone feels as if God is absent, and wonders, *Is this the time that I give it all up?*

One pastor, a former student of mine, told me how he would watch men who had been active in the congregation move week by week toward the back row of the church, sitting more and more toward the back until finally they no longer came. They had finally decided the church wasn't helping them deal with their lives, so they gave it up.

So I constantly pray that I will be sensitive to the one or two in my class who are on the edge.

● *Most are spiritually interested.* In every class, there will be bored people, like the husband who attended class only at his wife's insistence: he would fall asleep after my introductory remarks and awake as I concluded. A few others are in class because it's the religious thing to do, but they don't have a vital concern about God; they're just going through the motions.

I want, of course, to excite these people about Christ, but I also recognize that they constitute only a small percentage of the class. I don't want to focus the class on three or four uninterested people and miss the fifteen or twenty who are there to do business with God, for whom faith is a vital concern.

So as I prepare, I ask myself, *Who is the most likely to be responsive to what I have to give this week?*, and then I teach to those people. I think about the bored, and I try to entice them at various points in the class. But I won't let them tyrannize the lesson.

Illustrations that Cover the Canvas

Although I cannot hope to know and meet every concern in class, I can address a great variety. Naturally, the subject itself, whether Bible exposition or topical study, will answer a good many of the needs people bring to the class. But the other way I can insure that I touch a variety of people in a number of ways is by the effective use of illustrations. This means several things.

● *Use real situations.* Illustrations will connect with a variety of people if they speak about real human situations. I try not to use hypothetical illustrations — "If I were fired, I would . . ." because, though they show the relevant application, they never quite touch the heart. Nor do I often use dramatic examples, like Mother Theresa or Billy Graham, because their situations are so unlike those of my class.

I prefer that my illustrations come out of the life of the congregation. If I'm teaching on witnessing, I ask myself, *What does effective witnessing look like among these people?*

In one class, for instance, I talked about a woman who started caring for her elderly next door neighbor, bringing her lunch every day, doing some shopping for her. Eventually, she found herself sitting down with the woman and reading the Bible. She discovered that the woman had been active in the church some twenty or thirty years earlier. Slowly she was able to build faith into her friend.

Sometimes, of course, I may have to change some details to protect confidences. But I want the underlying story to be a genuine experience.

● *Slice them socially.* The above illustration makes sense to many women, but it wouldn't connect with many men. They are not likely to care about fixing lunch or doing shopping or sitting down in an intimate Bible discussion.

So in that class, I also talked about Bud, who did something similar with an 82-year-old woman in his neighborhood. Instead of fixing meals, he planted pachysandra in her front flower garden. He knew she had been an avid gardener and that she had taken great pride in that flower bed. But age had caught up to her and prevented her working in her garden. So for two months Bud spent his Saturday afternoons planting and weeding pachysandra for her.

In addition to targeting both men and women, I try to include some illustrations that work for couples and others for singles, some for those employed outside the home, others for those who work raising children in the home. I want to touch those who have children and those who don't, those in white collar and those in blue collar professions, whites and blacks and Asians and Hispanics.

In short, I want to use illustrations that come from the worlds represented in my classroom, for those worlds bear directly on people's emotional and spiritual lives. The illustrations may be but two sentences long, but the protagonist in the illustration will represent one of those groups. I don't have to touch every group at every point illustrated, but over the course of a class I want to hit all of them.

• *Slice them experientially*. I also try to slice my illustrations to cover the variety of experiences people have had.

If I want to illustrate how someone can be disappointed with God, I may be tempted to illustrate it mainly with the young mother of an infant and two toddlers who lost her husband to cancer. But not many people know that experience. So I may also mention other disappointments with God people experience: a young political activist who is upset about incipient racism, a man who didn't get a longed-for promotion, the teenager who didn't get accepted to the college of her choice.

Everybody experiences anger, grief, doubt, hope, pain, and love, but I can't assume that one illustration will cover every person's particular experience.

Keeping Methods in Their Place

In addition to their emotional and spiritual differences, people also learn in a variety of ways: some learn best by hearing, others by discussion; some by seeing, others by doing. Fortunately, we have a variety of teaching techniques that can connect with that type of variety. We can show a video or work with clay or break into small groups or do a "trust walk" to reinforce a lesson.

I don't want teaching methods, however, to become mere gimmicks to entertain people. And the way I prevent that is by asking myself three questions as I think about what method I want to use.

• *Does it tie in with the lesson?* I want people to enjoy learning, but I want the teaching technique to do more than help them appreciate learning. Any method I use must tie in directly to the goal of my lesson.

If I'm teaching Genesis 1, about creation, and I want people to experience the power of creativity, I'll have them write a poem or work with clay. If I want people to recognize afresh the beauty of creation, I'll pass around copies of *National Geographic* and ask them to pick out a picture that does that for them and have them talk about it. If I want people to get to know one another as a part of the lesson, I'll break them into small groups to talk about the most moving experience they've had outdoors. If I try switching these activities and my purpose, I may have an interesting class, but the class will not find the exercises very meaningful.

I also want people to be clear about how the exercise connects. People are generally conservative about trying something new, and they'll be thinking, *Why are we doing this?* So I usually tell them; "To help us understand some of what goes into creating, let's try this . . ."

Sometimes, of course, to explain this ruins the exercise — maybe the point of the exercise is to feel frustration due to ignorance! But if I've built trust by using meaningful exercises in the past, they'll trust me when they don't know exactly where the exercise is headed.

● *Is it proportionate to its importance?* I don't want to play an exercise for more than it's worth. If I do, I risk losing people, who will stop attending because they'll feel the class is too gimmicky.

I was supposed to attend a denominational gathering at which everyone was encouraged to come in wheelchairs; the judicatory wanted us to identify with the disabled. The problem was that the meeting typically ran six hours and included a meal. I didn't go. I think I would have gotten the point in about fifteen minutes, and yet the exercise was going to go on and on.

So, I want the exercise to be proportionate to the point being made. For instance, in studying Jesus' healing of the blind man, it may be helpful to have people identify with the blind man. If the lesson is finally about the light of Christ flooding our lives, it may be worthwhile to take twenty to thirty minutes to do a "trust walk," where people break into twos and take turns leading one another around the church, the led person being blindfolded. Then people can grasp in a fresh way the transformation Christ works in us.

If, however, I want to emphasize the obedience of the blind man following his healing, spending so much time on identifying with his affliction would be inappropriate, distracting the class from the main point.

• *Is the class ready for it?* The number and type of teaching methods I employ depends on the nature of the people I'm teaching.

For example, if I'm teaching a class composed of men and women in their fifties, somewhat conservative, I'm not going to work with clay or write poetry, even if it fits in with the goal of the lesson. That group's traditional expectations for what is supposed to happen in a class would get in the way of their enjoying the new technique.

If I'm teaching singles between the ages of 25 and 35, who want to build relationships and enjoy being creative, I can be much more innovative — in fact, I have to be. They would find traditional teaching unchallenging.

I can often shape an exercise so that it fits the group I'm working with. I'll ask myself, *What would I have to do to make this work in this setting?* If most of the class wants meaty lecture, I will shorten the discussion period so they won't get bored. If I know that a number of parents will leave the class ten minutes early to pick up their children from Sunday school, I'll offer the discussion at the beginning of class. If my "conservative" group happens to be composed of many choir members, I may be able to get away with using music in class. But I will work hard at making sure the exercise and the group fit.

• *Is it dessert or the main course?* People enjoy being surprised, and one of my goals in teaching is to remain somewhat unpredictable. That's been especially important when I've been in a church for more than five years. If I'm not careful, people will be able to finish my sentences for me.

But, in an effort to keep people alert, I don't want to offer so many creative exercises that they become the main course of the class. I usually use no more than one new exercise in a class and may not introduce one for four or five weeks.

I know I'm beginning to depend on exercises when I feel I need to do something to fill time. Instead, I want to have two hours of content prepared for every hour I have to teach, and I want the exercise to be so vital that I really can't go on with other material until the point I'm driving at is made clear in some fresh way. That's when I know the new method is the dessert and not the main dish.

When I offer variety without gimmicks, I'm able to present a class in ways that will touch people of different learning styles. I employ many exercises, especially group discussion. Here are a few others I have also found helpful.

Visual Variety

Because we live in a culture dominated by the visual, I rarely fail to include some visual element in a class.

For me, that usually means using overheads or printed lecture outlines. First, I can prepare some overheads at home — I don't have to slow down the teaching by writing during class. Second, when I do want to write during the session, I never have to turn my back to the class; I can maintain eye contact. And third, using overheads helps people *see* what we're talking about; that way they can keep more ideas in mind as I teach.

For example, I may ask the class what they think when they hear the word "justification." If I write their answers as they give them, they can keep all of them in mind, comparing, contrasting as we go. That's especially helpful when we begin talking about Paul's views.

Visual can also mean using a video tape in class, although I don't find it helpful to use videos for more than five or ten minutes; otherwise they tend to jar the dynamics of class interaction, making people a little more passive than I'm comfortable with. But I've sometimes used brief portions of commercials or TV shows to drive home a point.

I also use handouts, either material I've prepared or magazines or articles. For instance, I was teaching from 2 Corinthians on making every thought obedient to Christ. So I passed out sections of the newspaper — real estate, fashion, front page — and asked people to discuss the Christian implications of what they saw.

Tactile Teaching

Many people don't learn well unless their sense of touch or smell is put to use. So when the subject is conducive, I will include a tactile exercise.

In studying the creation story once, I had the class try to make a human figure out of clay. Then I asked them questions like "What goes into creating?" and "What do you have to do to create?" Having worked with the clay, the class was much more sensitive to the dynamics of creation.

Writing is the simplest tactile exercise. So I often ask people to write something in response to a question. Other times I'll ask people to circle the most significant words in the passage we're studying. I don't know why, but there is something about writing that focuses the mind.

I once brought in perfumes when teaching 2 Corinthians 2:16: "To the one we are the smell of death; to the other, the fragrance of life." And in order to grasp better Paul's discussion of the veil in chapter 3, I've had the class experiment seeing through a veil.

As I mentioned, I don't do this type of thing often lest it become gimmicky. But when used appropriately, it not only adds variety to the class, it helps those who learn best through their senses.

Tuning in with Music

I was teaching 1 John at a week-long family camp for members of our church. I wanted people to memorize key verses and ideas of the book, so as we went along chapter by chapter, I taught people a hymn or Scripture song that summarized the teaching or helped them memorize a verse. In fact, we sang them as we moved through the week.

I still have people from that retreat who tell me how helpful those sessions were. Some come up to me and just start singing, "Behold what manner of love the Father has given unto us . . ."

In a class on world missions, we adopted a theme song of challenge and commitment. The stirring words and music sealed the course content in our hearts.

Music is a vital part of worship because it helps us give praise to God, the main point of worship. But music can be used in a classroom as well.

Use of Imagination

Actually, nearly every creative teaching technique requires people to draw on their imaginations, but sometimes the attempt is more direct.

For instance, I've had a friend draw a cartoon, but I'll ask the class to write a caption for it. And even though three-fourths of the class doesn't come up with anything, we end up with two or three captions that illustrate the point wonderfully.

I've also used guided imagery, or guided imagination. Again you have to know your audience and have to be very careful with it, but it can be used effectively to help people identify with a biblical situation.

Once when teaching about the healing of the blind man outside of Jericho, I said, "Now close your eyes and imagine you are a member of the crowd. What does it feel like? Is it hot or is it cold? Hot. Okay, it's hot. Is it rainy or, no, it's dry and it's dusty. Well, what does it feel like when a lot of people are milling around? Now you hear a cry, 'Jesus, Son of David, have mercy on me.' What are you thinking?" And on it goes.

I want to do more than just talk about healing but also help people experience that reality. Imagination helps do that.

The Power of Silence

Some people can grasp new truths only when they have time to reflect on them silently. So in some classes, I use silence as a teaching technique, especially carefully guided biblical meditation.

When I've taught from Psalm 62, "For God alone my soul awaits in silence," I've asked people to take five minutes and meditate on the word *wait*. "You can use the time in any way you want," I'll say. "You may move off to a corner of the room or stay where you are. Write your thoughts down if you want. If you have no idea what to do, let me suggest you think on these things: How well do you do at waiting? What do you think it means to wait for God?"

Before that, we've talked about waiting for the check in the mail, waiting for Prince Charming to rescue us, waiting for Christmas, despairing while we wait. So they'll have mental furniture to work with during the exercise.

Meditation can be a moving exercise for some people, so I don't want to end it abruptly. At the end I will close with prayer and gently move that class back into the normal ebb and flow of conversation, beginning the prayer softly and slowly, ending in a normal pace and tone of voice.

There's power in silence. There can also be anxiety. If there's anxiety, I hear it in coughing, fidgeting, moving. I will shorten the period, and then after class I'll think of a way to help people handle it better the next time: perhaps introduce it more thoroughly, explain the biblical base for meditation, or use a less threatening meditation.

Creating Learning Space

Recently, I was speaking with a group of students at Eastern College, when one of them asked me, "Shouldn't everybody on this campus have the same view about how Christianity relates to justice and lifestyle in American culture?"

"No, I don't see it that way," I said. "We all need to be centered in Christ and under the authority of Scripture, but within those boundaries we have the freedom to ask questions and wrestle with the shape of our obedience to God."

When the meeting broke up, a student approached me and said, "I've come from a background where everybody told me what I had to think and believe about everything, including politics and lifestyle. Frankly, it was starting to make me less of a Christian. I cannot tell you what it means to hear you say that here I am given space to explore what I really believe. Thank you."

I not only want to give people space to ask questions but also space to seek answers in a variety of ways. Just as there are no biblical directions to some aspects of our faith — like whether to part our hair on the right or left — so there is no one right way to learn about Christ.

I think that's why Jesus constantly employed variety in his teaching. He cursed fig trees, knelt, drew in the dirt, made mud, pointed to the lilies, among other things. He knew that not everyone learns alike.

I have the same goal for both older and newer Christians: to make the language fresh, to make it come alive. Both groups need to see how exciting the text is, how filled with meaning it is.

— Earl Palmer

CHAPTER FIVE

Baby Lambs and Old Sheep

Becky, a new Christian in my Bible class, sparkles with enthusiasm even though she needs help to find Galatians: "Is that Old or New Testament?" she asks. I could tell her, "Jesus loves me, this I know," and she would be awed by the depth of my teaching.

Tim, on the other hand, raised in the church, has heard it all before. He's tired of "Jesus Loves Me" and may have read Galatians ten times already.

The problem is, they both sit in the same Bible study I teach.

School teachers have specific assignments: "Ninth-grade

English literature." Pastors can't be so specific. I wonder what school teachers would do with a task like the pastor's: teach 200 students, kindergarten to graduate school (some gifted, some slow), covering everything from colors and the alphabet to biochemistry and calculus.

That is the challenge put before the pastor, to teach a diverse group of people who possess a variety of skills.

The easy way out, of course, is to offer classes for the new believer and classes for the mature believer. And there is a place for that.

But most of the time I prefer them to attend the same Bible study together. It's refreshing for mature Christians to see younger Christians excitedly discover old truths. It not only reminds them of the eternal freshness of the gospel, it also gives them new ways of seeing old truths.

New believers, on the other hand, need to hear the wisdom and experience that older Christians offer. It gives them the long view and helps stabilize their lives.

Though the benefits are great, teaching a mixed class of old and new Christians, where you can bore the mature or overwhelm the neophyte, requires skill and sound technique.

The Diverse Challenge

As I set out to teach both new and mature Christians together, I must be aware of temptations and roadblocks that may get in the way of effective teaching.

● *Temptations to avoid.* With mature believers, who may be on the verge of boredom because they think they know it all, I may be tempted to try to make the Bible more interesting. So I may think that a study of the esoteric, like the Book of Revelation or first-century Gnosticism, might work best.

Certainly subjects like these are worthy of attention, but I must not be lured into discussing them while ignoring the heart of the gospel, for that is perennially the most interesting part of *our message.* Teachers who say, "We need to give these people some really tough courses on some big, major themes," deprive the older person of the challenge of a simple treatment of the biblical text. Most of the time, the older Christian needs the explosive experience of seeing 1 John in a fresh way.

One temptation in talking with new believers is to rely on clichés or to give them generalized truths to memorize. Worse still is to ask them simplistic questions, where they just fill in the blanks after reading a verse. In short, I mustn't insult their intelligence.

Another temptation with new believers is let them bask in their new experience as Christians. We do that when we teach them to share their faith on the basis of their experience: "I was troubled, and now Christ has brought me peace." That may be true, but lots of people get peace, some from crack cocaine or Eastern religions.

Instead of exploiting their subjective experience, then, I want instead to ground them in the Bible, so that they will have a firm basis for sharing their faith.

● *Roadblocks to overcome.* Young believers often feel awkward or doubtful about their new role; they know others have been around longer and know more. They feel silly asking if Galatians is Old Testament or New.

This lack of confidence can undermine their ability to grow in Christ, especially to study the Bible — it is, after all, a huge book, in some ways unwieldly and complicated. So I want new Christians to feel friendly toward the Bible, to gain confidence that they can use the Bible themselves, to feel the Bible is their book.

Older Christians are roadblocked not by lack of experience but by experience itself. For instance, some get roadblocked in the prophetic mode: they can't get beyond the Bible's teachings about the need for justice and our responsibility to the poor. Others may be roadblocked by evangelism: they can't see anything but a call to evangelize. At some point, such people have heard a sermon or had an experience that significantly shapes their outlook and hinders them from seeing the full sweep of the gospel.

Others are roadblocked by bad experiences: their encounters with extreme charismatics, for instance, may make them unwilling to consider openly the role of the Holy Spirit in their lives. Or an unanswered prayer may make them cynical about prayer.

So for older Christians, I have to help them see beyond the roadblock, to expose them to the full dimensions of the Christian faith.

The Common Response

It would appear that these diverse challenges would demand diverse responses on the part of the teacher. In some ways, yes, so the teacher should keep this diversity in mind and shape the study accordingly.

Yet, in the end, the way to meet these temptations and overcome these roadblocks is the same: inductive Bible study.

The wonderful thing about the Bible is that it is a great discipleship tool no matter where we are in our journey. Given the chance, the Bible molds and shapes us, and remolds and reshapes us for a lifetime. Young believers have limited information — a lot of the language, categories, images, and symbols of faith are unknown to them. But older Christians have essentially the same problem: they have information, but they often don't understand the information they have. Underconfidence or overconfidence simply compounds the problem.

So, I have the same goal for both groups — to make the language fresh, to make it come alive, helping them discover what it means. Both groups need to see how exciting the text is, how filled with meaning it is.

I've found that happens especially when I let the Bible speak for itself, when I study it inductively, not coming at it with preconceived categories, but attempting to discover what it says about itself.

Journey into the Word One Step at a Time

Inductive study alone, of course, is no magic key. I still have to shape the study so that it helps people see the text in a fresh way. I use a number of techniques to do that, the first of which is studying short passages — and just those passages.

For example, I might play this game with my class. "I'm a

Roman soldier living in the first century," I'll say. "Late one night, a young man with a scroll tucked under his arm comes running down an alley. He looks suspicious, so I grab for him, but he's too quick. All I get is a little piece of his manuscript. So I take the evidence in to headquarters. They fold it neatly and send it over to the Roman CIA, Caesar's Intelligence Agency, because they want to know what kind of a document might be carried by a mysterious runner in the middle of the night. The agent unfolds the scrap of manuscript and spreads it out under the light of his lamp.

"Now, if you were that CIA agent and that piece of scroll —the first few verses of Philippians — was all you had to work with, what could you tell me from the document? Why was it written? What kind of people was it written to? What do they believe? What are they trying to do?"

For instance, if they had a scrap of Philippians 1, they would see Paul writing to the church at Philippi with its deacons and bishops — so they would discover the church is organized. They would see the name *Jesus Christ* used frequently in just a few verses — so whoever Jesus is, he's important to this movement. In fact, he's called Lord, and that means something in any century.

I don't care how much or how little Bible knowledge people have, this kind of approach creates an incredible Bible study experience. It enables Christians — novices or veterans — to do an inductive Bible study together. New believers have as much to work with as the older ones. The Sunday school expert who's memorized dozens of verses can't interject some oblique thought by saying, "Well over in John it says this and over in Luke it says this." He's restricted to focus on a particular scrap of material.

Forced to concentrate on a single portion, older Christians also make new discoveries. They thought they understood the passage so well, but they now realize, "Hey! I'm seeing new things."

Help People See the Word

Another method I've used helps people see the text, literally: I have them draw or doodle.

This is especially useful with youth. For instance, I've put a huge piece of butcher paper on the floor with, let's say, Mark 1-3 written at the top. I give a passage of those chapters to each pair of kids and tell them to draw a picture of what's happening in it.

Then we walk along the butcher paper, section by section, and talk about what the kids drew. In that way, they're not only hearing the words, they're also visualizing the text. And they see a sequence of events, especially when we're in the Gospels or the Book of Acts.

I've done similar things with adults. I'm a great believer in people doodling when I'm teaching. With people sitting at a table, each with some paper, I might say, "Before we discuss this passage, make some stick men and stick women — draw a picture of what you see happening here." Or I might ask them to make one simple drawing reflecting what they saw in the text. Then I ask those who are willing to explain their doodling to the others.

This works not just for the Gospels, but the letters of the New Testament as well. Paul's letters, for instance, are full of imagery (thorn in the flesh, crucified with Christ, running the race, etc.) as are other so-called didactic portions of the Bible.

Such a procedure not only reveals the vividness of the text, it puts everyone, new believer and old, on the same level. When people are saying, "This is what I saw" or "This is what I felt," there are no experts. There is no right or wrong answer to such questions.

Naturally, I want to take them beyond this level, because in the end the text has something to teach us. There are right and wrongs we must learn to distinguish between. But I begin by helping everyone start the journey to the deeper level from the same place.

Let the Text Define the Words

One of the responsibilities of the teacher is, as C. S. Lewis put it, to tell people "what the hard words mean." That is also a good way to teach a class mixed with new and mature believers.

How do I do that? First, I ask my twentieth-century readers for their own definitions. "What do you think of when you hear that word *grace?*" Every person is going to have experience with that word, and experience is neutral.

In addition, as discussion ensues, I'm able to determine what baggage, background, and understandings people bring to the word. Then I can better compare or contrast the use of the word in its own setting.

Second, we study the use of the word in the text itself. Since I usually limit our study to the text at hand, this gives everyone equal access to the primary source material. No one can intimidate others with specialized knowledge. In fact, I find that specialized knowledge is usually not that helpful anyway. A skillful teacher in the inductive method can help a class see the meaning of the word 90 percent of the time by simply examining carefully the word in its context.

Take for instance, the word for *love, agape*. The apostle Paul defines that word himself by the way he uses it. 1 Corinthians 13 is the most famous example. A new believer can be coached line by line through that chapter and consequently gain an understanding for biblical love. The same exercise done by an older believer would uncover practical implications about love that most believers have yet to negotiate in their own lives.

It can startle veteran Christians, for example, as they take that chapter sentence by sentence and suddenly realize they can do a loving thing — give all they possess to the poor — and still not do it out of love. So the impact of the meaning of words in a text can affect both the new and the older Christian.

For this to happen, however, we must take the time to allow the text to reveal itself. We cannot jump in to define words too quickly. I try to create an atmosphere that enhances discovery. Bible studies or sermons become boring to older Christians if they think they already know what the words mean when they really don't. Bible studies become boring when we don't allow the text to develop, unfolding in a natural progression of thought.

Old and New Sheep Feed On the Same Pasture

My experience has shown me that when the average young Christian and the typical older Christian get a chance to see the text unfold in a way that's fresh, they're wide open to Bible study and eager for it. A young person — maybe not even a Christian — who thinks the Bible isn't interesting or is impossible to understand can become fascinated by a new approach to the Bible. And it can happen right alongside the veteran Christian who has been bored and uninterested because he thinks he knows it all already.

Recently I climbed Mount Shasta with a brilliant young lawyer. The night before the climb, sitting under the stars, he told me his story.

He was highly educated, involved in New Age thinking, married to a woman from a non-Christian religion, father of three lovely children, successful in his career, yet he knew he was adrift. He had abandoned his religious upbringing and knew he lacked something necessary and central to his life.

Someone steered him our direction, and he started coming to church two years ago. "In one sermon," he told me later, "you started to explain a word from the Bible, and I cried because I realized I didn't know what that word was, and I wanted to know so badly."

Now here's a guy who thought he knew what church was all about because he had gone through a parochial school system. In that sense he was like an old sheep, but in another sense he was a new sheep. But it doesn't matter, because I've come to see that the fundamental need for each group is the same.

At the base of Mount Shasta my young friend helped me discover the tremendous power of people's appetite for God. They will devour biblical truth that's alive and fresh.

Successful teaching not only opens the mind but also stirs
the emotions, fires the imagination, galvanizes the will.
— Howard Hendricks

CHAPTER SIX

Teaching That Motivates

While milling around at conferences, I occasionally bump into pastors who say to me, "Prof, you once changed the whole course of my life."

"Fantastic!" I reply. "How did it happen?"

"Years ago in class you made one statement that opened my eyes to a whole new perspective on ministry."

I never cease to marvel how powerful truth is — even one sentence of truth — and how profoundly teachers can motivate others. Successful teaching not only opens the mind but also stirs the emotions, fires the imagination, galvanizes the will. If I didn't embrace that, I would despair, for I live not just to teach truth but to change people.

Of course, motivational teaching isn't necessarily the norm. I've heard some Quaalude teaching in my days that left my mind more in a torpor than a tempest. What is the difference between that and stimulating teaching? How can teachers motivate their students?

Help Listeners Identify with You

My wife belongs to a fraternity of journalists that some time ago sponsored a talk by playwright Arthur Miller. She got two tickets, and I jumped at the chance to go with her. After his presentation, Miller invited questions.

"Mr. Miller," someone asked, "How can you tell when you have a good play?"

"When I sit in the audience during one of my plays," he answered, "and in the midst of it I want to shout, 'That's me!' then I know I've got a good one."

Miller has hit on one of the most important principles not only of great plays, but of motivating teaching: our soul is moved by what we can identify with.

People want to see themselves: their dreams, their needs, their problems, and their heartbreaks. Nothing moves listeners more than their reality, their experience, their emotions, their struggles. They don't want to hear something brand new as much as something relevant to them. They want to feel, *This teacher understands me.*

There are several things we can do to help people identify with us.

● *Tell it like it is.* Shun euphemisms, candy coating, fluff, party line. Few identify with baloney and PR. Telling it like it isn't alienates people. On the other hand, direct, honest speech is powerful.

I have enjoyed good results speaking at men's conferences, and I think being straightforward is the reason. Men respond to horseradish. They want gutsy, realistic truth.

I'm not advocating shock teaching but forthright teaching. People identify with real-world advice, not utopian, spin-control sayings. They're less interested in the way things are supposed to be than in the way they are.

For instance, when I talk about our culture's growing taste for tainted entertainment, I could describe that in gentle terms: calmly citing statistics to show that violence and perverted sex sell better in the movies than wholesome films, or that Madonna or Roseanne Barr outdraw Bill Cosby or Bob Hope. Instead, I usually prefer something more earthy: "We live in a society that can't tell the difference between Chanel No. 5 and Sewer Gas No. 9."

● *Major in human interest material.* Pastor and author Chuck Swindoll devours the writings of Erma Bombeck, who is a master of the commonplace. She majors in Everyday, where Bob and Linda live 99 percent of their lives. It's no surprise that people identify with her.

So I try to relate my teaching to the frustration parents feel about their preschoolers, the discouragement business people feel in their careers, the anxiety young couples have about money, the crazy and cute things kids do, the fun of playing softball.

● *Share your own struggles.* After attending one seminar, a friend said to me, "I wish just once the teacher would have admitted he had sinned or at least had a tough time. Either he plays in a different league, or I don't know what the Christian life is all about."

A super pious, ultra spiritual teacher often does more to discourage people than to motivate them. By the end, listeners feel, *I guess I just don't have it. I can't cut it. I could never be like that.*

On the other hand, I find whenever I share a failure or mistake, my students come out of the rocks to tell me how much it meant to them. Suddenly they feel, *Hey, there's hope for me.*

I'm not talking about an emotional strip tease, revealing things that are intimate, but teaching as if I don't have everything down pat. The approach is "Look, I don't have all of the answers about prayer, but I'm sure involved in the process. Let me share what God is teaching me about this." When we do, as Arthur Miller put it, people will think, *That's me! He's describing me!*

We can still share successes. Otherwise we're just the blind leading the blind. Talking about our successes brings credibility. Still, the tone is: "I am someone in process rather than the finished product; yes, I have some successes, but I haven't always been this way."

● *Build rapport.* The more I am involved with my students, the greater my long-term impact on them. Sure, there are a few initiators who simply take what I say and run with it. But most of my students need personal contact and rapport with the teacher.

Establishing rapport isn't difficult or mysterious; it's a matter of getting to know students and letting them know me. Even if the teacher is vastly different in personality and interests, listeners will identify with the teacher if he or she acts like a friend.

So I don't cloister myself in the office; I make it a point to get out on the campus. That's why they named the benches around here "Prof's benches;" that's where I often talk to students. I also go to the student center and lunch with them.

And I start the conversation anywhere, usually with a variation of "What's going on in your life?" Before long the student will be asking questions, and sometimes I end up doing more teaching there than in the classroom. But the main result is this: because of the rapport we've built, that student identifies with me and is more likely to be motivated in the classroom.

● *Use humor.* One time a bell interrupted a choice discussion in class. I looked at the clock and grimaced, "Sometimes I wish I could shoot that thing off the wall!" About a week later at the end of another class session I warned, "We're going to get caught by that clock again!" A student stood up and fired a rubber arrow at the face of the clock while the class roared in laughter. I played it to the hilt.

Humor helps people identify with a teacher for many reasons. People bond when they agree about what's funny. Humor also gently and indirectly shows people's foibles. And humor puts everyone on common ground.

Since daily life is filled with humorous circumstances, people have trouble identifying with someone who is unfailingly serious. Humor shows that you're real. So even though my topic may be serious, I make it a point to sugar it with humor.

Express Confidence in Learners

Chuck Swindoll, who studied under me at Dallas Seminary, once said to me, "The thing I appreciated most about you was you believed in me when I didn't believe in myself." He says I wrote on one of his papers, "Chuck, if you continue to write like this, some day you may become a great writer." Chuck was always a disciplined guy, with loads of enthusiasm, but for whatever reason, partly his upbringing, partly his own self-image, he just didn't believe he could do it. It didn't take any genius on my part to see the flashes of greatness in him. But it did take my willingness to express confidence in someone who at that point only had potential.

Affirmation has a tremendous power to motivate people to learn and even achieve great things. And I've found when I follow seven guidelines, my affirmation has its greatest impact.

1. Base it on fact. When affirming learners, we can't blow smoke. That backfires every time. If we toss out kudos indiscriminately, eventually we lose credibility. Furthermore, mention specific things that indicate progress or potential: not "I like your work" but "Your writing is punchy and clear."

2. Begin with the positives. Teachers and preachers often get in a critiquing rut; we're often bothered by the negatives and unimpressed with the positives.

Negatives need to be mentioned, of course, but in due time. For example, more than the twenty-seven things wrong with his sermon, a learning preacher first needs to know the two things he did right. He's got to start somewhere.

After I've convinced him, "Man, you've got these two things going for you," thus motivating him to continue, then I can say, "Would you like to know something that will help make you better?" I've never met anyone who refused.

3. Repeat the affirmation. I met Tom Landry when he was coach of the Dallas Cowboys. Having observed that he had more walk-ons who became all-pros than any other coach, I asked how he did it.

"First, you've got to see potential," he said. "But I don't stop there; I start there. Then I keep telling them that they're going to have to bust their tail to get that potential into action."

I've never forgotten what he said next: "I discovered that I've got to repeat to a player over and over again what his strength is. He may hear me but not to the extent that he needs to hear me. I keep telling him, 'You can, you can, you can.' "

You can't break a student's habit of negative thinking overnight or with one compliment. For years they have been thinking hundreds and thousands of negative thoughts. They are deeply ingrained — and reinforced by their failures, which will happen to anyone. In addition, even as we affirm learners, new failures keep on coming and weaknesses will endure. Only ongoing, repeated affirmation can counteract that.

4. Encourage learners to set their own goals. Once students have their momentum going, I try to motivate them to outdo me. I can't do everything well, but I can motivate others to realize their gifts and potential in Christ, kicking them out of the nest and urging them not only to fly, but to soar.

One day after class a student asked if I could give him something more challenging. I assured him I could and called a friend at the Juvenile Detention Home: "I have a student who needs an education."

"I get the picture," he assured me.

At the center they put the young man into a cell with an offender convicted of numerous counts of delinquency.

"Hey, what's your line," the delinquent sneered. "Every day they send somebody in here with a different line. What's yours?"

Afterward my student returned to the seminary and said to me, "That was tough. I need all the help I can get in that type of situation. Can you recommend any materials?" So we sat down and worked out a personal reading program to stretch him toward his higher goals.

5. Affirm publicly. I attended First Baptist in Dallas one day when Pastor Criswell called a woman from the congregation to the pulpit. "I'd like you people to know," he said, "that Mary has been teaching in our junior department for seven years. And I just got a report that in the last month three girls have come to know Jesus Christ in her class." The whole congregation broke into applause.

This not only gave the teacher a boost, I could just see people thinking, *Where do I sign up?*

6. *Get excited about their discoveries.* We express confidence in learners by treating them with respect. For the teacher, that means taking seriously the ideas and discoveries of students. If we speak enthusiastically about what we know but indifferently about the student's insight, we make them feel like dummies. We undermine their confidence in what they can understand about the Bible, sucking the wind out of their sails.

Instead, I treat students as though they are incredibly smart. I work up a heavier lather over what the learners are discovering than over what I have discovered. I write all over their papers, hold them up, and tell others, "You've got to read this!"

Although I may have learned the same thing thirty years ago, I get as excited as if I myself were making the same discovery. And I'm not putting on a show. I sincerely thrill over seeing learners learn.

7. *Highlight potential.* Not only competence but *potential* competence motivates. If I know there are skills in me that lay like an undrilled oilfield, I will be stirred to start some wells and get pumping. Recognized potential enables learners to say, "Yes, I'm stumbling around now, but someday I will be a good parent," or "Someday I will win others to Christ," or "Someday I will be able to counsel others.

During my student years at Wheaton College, my most motivating teacher was Merrill Tenney. I know why he kindled such fire: he believed in me and communicated that confidence. One time he put his arm around me and said, "Howie, I believe God has a great future for you, and I want you to know I'm 100 percent on your team." Here I was, a kid still wet behind the ears; here he was, a great New Testament scholar — and he believed in me. He saw potential. That drove me on to higher things. I wanted to fulfill what he saw in me.

Equip People with Skills

We conducted studies at Dallas Seminary and elsewhere, and found that the number one problem among students is a lack of confidence. They are hindered, paralyzed, and discouraged by insecurity. Yet these are high caliber people, serious students with a B minus average and above, graduates of quality schools.

I think they are a product of our culture. Confidence comes not from easy living but from overcoming adversity. Most of our students have known the good life; they haven't endured a major economic depression or overcome a significant personal adversity. Few have faced anything that tested them to the core of their being, that stretched them to the maximum, to the point where they had to rely totally on God.

Motivation comes from the confidence that "I can do everything through him who gives me strength." Paul said those words in Philippians *after* describing in the preceding verses all the adverse circumstances he had overcome with God's help. Paul had proven to himself that God could work through him.

That's why wilderness camping experiences such as Outward Bound have helped so many youth in this generation. After jumping off a two-hundred-foot cliff and rappelling to the bottom, they hit the ground a new person. It's a way of giving them what life hasn't: great challenges and new skills packaged in a short span of time.

Thus, motivational teaching will always be concerned not only with ought-to's but also how-to's. Ought-to's without how-to's actually demoralize people by making them feel increasingly like failures. It's like showing movies of a world championship football team to novice football players and saying, "You should do that," without coaching the skills needed to pull it off. The distance between where they are and where they should be is too wide, with no identifiable pathway to the top. Skills and competency encourage by showing the path.

For example, the average man avoids reading and studying the Bible primarily because he doesn't know how. He would like to know firsthand what God says, but he presumes the Bible is for the professionals, the pastors, the capable. He's *just* a carpenter, a salesman, a truck driver, a businessman. So he learns to occupy himself around the church in ways he won't make a fool out of himself — ushering, cutting the lawn.

Years ago I taught the members of the Dallas Cowboy football team to study the Bible. I remember Roger Staubach, the all-pro quarterback, objecting, "Hey, I think you've got the wrong group. We've got too many linemen in here." He was wrong; they ate it up. Dan Reeves, an assistant coach, came up after one session and said, "Doc, I learned more in one hour in this class than I've learned all my life. How come?"

Because I had simply equipped him with skills so he could study the Bible for himself.

Speak to Needs

What spurs a teacher to teach and what motivates a student to learn are usually two very different things. Teachers often find inspiration in a body of knowledge or experiences, significant truths that they want others to know about. Learners, on the other hand, are generally motivated by their felt needs; that's usually the grid through which they see the world. As a result, teachers are often answering questions that learners aren't asking.

However, teachers never lack motivated learners when they speak to needs. The greater people's pain, the greater their motivation to learn. With their marriage crumbling, a couple will be compelled to hear a sermon series on family peace, but they would likely give only half a mind to a series on "Reconciling God's Sovereignty and Human Freedom."

But felt needs — for a new job, for a less hectic life, for a harmonious family — are frequently only symptoms of ultimate needs — for meaning, for security, for companionship. The Bible specializes in ultimate needs. The motivating teacher surfaces those ultimate needs and ties them to felt needs.

For example, a man paralyzed by fear may crave assurances that he will not lose his job, but his real need is to trust God to never forsake him. If I make it clear that by knowing God better he will overcome fear and anxiety, he will have a much higher level of trust, even if the job does indeed evaporate.

Many teachers are good speakers but poor listeners. I encourage pastors to take churchgoers out for breakfast, ask questions, and keep quiet: "What's going on in your life? What are you losing sleep over? What are you disagreeing with your wife about? Where do you feel inadequate? What are you struggling with?"

Laypersons often feel pastors descend from heaven on Sunday morning and ascend on Sunday night, that they don't live on this planet. When you preach on subjects based on conversations, people will think you've been reading their mail. One man whose pastor had done this said to me, "My pastor has had a brush with reality."

Even something as abstract as doctrinal teaching can be approached from needs. Few in our day could care less about theology, but whether they know it or not, they do care passionately about it. When a man's wife has just died, he is vitally interested in the subject of the sovereignty of God. He just might not be able to phrase his need that way.

Therefore, I've found it best to teach theology by a case-study approach, relating life situations to specific doctrines. For me theology is not the study of a seamless, systematic body of knowledge but of answers to life's most troubling questions.

And when I can convince people that in the Bible they will discover truths that will change their life for the good, make them better people, answer their questions, and guide their decisions, they will be inflamed to learn it.

In the end, motivating teachers are good listeners. John Stott said that teachers need to be not only students of what they have to teach but of what their listeners need to learn.

But there is one more element. As John Stott once said to me, "I've discovered it's not hard to be biblical if you don't care about being contemporary. And it's certainly not hard to be contemporary if you don't care about being biblical. Being biblical and contemporary — that's the art of Christian communication."

And that's also the key to motivating people to learn.

I've always felt that the heartbeat of the church is adults.
Jesus loved children, but he did not call children. He
called adults.

— Roberta Hestenes

CHAPTER SEVEN

The Unique Task of Teaching Adults

Some years ago, I knew a Christian attorney who was appointed by the church board to be chairman of the adult education program. He was perfectly willing to oversee the program. He was willing to teach. He was a good teacher. But he was completely unwilling to take a course. I asked him why.

"I learned everything I need to know about the Christian faith when I was a kid in Sunday school," he replied. "Now I'm an adult and the challenge is to live what I already know."

To him adult education was remedial, for adults who somehow missed getting a Christian education when they were younger.

This is not an uncommon view. It arises, in part, from the common attitude toward all education in our culture, that schooling is something you do when you are young. At a certain point you graduate and you are all done with education. Even worse, the attitude upon graduation may be *Thank goodness I don't have to do that anymore!*

Often our Sunday schools, confirmation classes, and youth programs parallel the public education experience so that we send the subliminal message, *Education is for children. The sooner you're through with it the better.*

But that attitude can be turned around. When I first came to one church, there were fewer than 200 people in Sunday morning classes out of a congregation of 4,000. That meant only 5 percent of the congregation was involved in adult education.

Eventually we found ways to increase involvement to 1,000 adults, or about 25 percent involvement — still not phenomenal, but better. Obviously a significant number of adults began to change their view of adult education.

Here, then, are a few insights that have guided me as I've worked with adults in various educational settings, ideas that not only have helped adults get involved but have changed lives as well.

The Importance of Adult Education

To begin with, I've had to remind myself and the churches with which I've worked about the importance of adult education. Often children and youth education gets top billing in congregations, and for good reason. But often that's at the expense of adults.

Without slighting the importance of children and young people, I've always felt that the heartbeat of the church is adults. Jesus loved children, but he did not call children as his disciples. He called adults. We have no example in the Gospels of Jesus teaching children. But we have many, many stories of Jesus teaching adults.

Furthermore, it is adults who shape the world, for good or ill, and it is adult Christians who are called to be salt and light in a dying world. It is adults who vote. It is adults who work and who control the governments, schools, corporations, unions, social groups, charities, and other institutions of our society. It is adults who are called to actively disciple their own families. It is adults who decide the church's priorities and budgets. To teach adults is to be on the firing line of Christian ministry and social change.

Consequently, when we address adults, we can address some significant issues. For example, I find that many Christian men as they reach mid-life are troubled by issues of boredom in marriage, disillusionment with the church, and suffering that seems to have no purpose.

But often they ponder these questions alone, in silence, with no one to empathize or even listen to them. In adult education, we have the important privilege of helping people understand their fears and work through tough issues with a mature biblical perspective. We can touch the throbbing pulse of human pain, anxiety, hope, and joy.

The problem, as my lawyer friend showed me, is that many people in churches today have never brought their adult minds to bear on an understanding of the Bible. They tend to assume that Scripture has nothing specific or helpful to say to them about the real world in which they live. For them, the Bible seems like a relic from childhood rather than a living statement of hard-edged truths that demand to be studied and interacted with on a daily basis.

But the Bible was written primarily for adults, to answer adult questions, to deal with adult problems. Finally, then, adult education is vital to the church because it is our opportunity to open the Word of God, the textbook of the church, for people to whom it is ultimately addressed.

Who Are the Adults We Teach?

Adults learn differently than do children, and I've found it helpful to keep in mind the unique characteristics of adult learners whenever I've taught adults. Malcolm Knowles, in his *The Practice of Modern Adult Education*, has given me a lot of insight here.

● *The adult learner is self-directed.* Adults like to see themselves as self-directed and in charge of their own lives. But sometimes we inadvertently make them feel dependent, almost like children.

For example, when you put people in rows in a classroom, many adults feel (even if only subconsciously) that they are in a childlike setting. Since many people look back on their school days in a less than positive way, the return to a classroom as an adult can have unhappy connotations.

Furthermore, few adults will volunteer to be placed in situations where they will feel they are being talked down to or treated with condescension. When the teacher is the "expert" and the learner is "talked at," the adult hardly feels in charge of the learning environment.

Some adults, of course, have no problem with such a model of learning, but most adults rebel and vote with their feet; they find another class — or even another church — where they are not made to feel like they've stumbled back into Miss Grimble's sixth-grade class.

● *The adult learner has accumulated a large reservoir of experiences.* As adults grow, they learn to trust their own judgment and experience more and more, and they test what they hear from others against their own sampling of reality. If what the teacher says is not validated by and connected with their own experience, they will not take the teacher's message seriously.

We are wise if we can put this experience to good use in the classroom. For example, once I wanted to develop a course for blended families. At first, I thought of inviting an "expert" (say, a psychologist) to teach the course. But I decided to draw on the experience of the people who might attend such a class.

So I invited some blended families to meet with me, and I asked them questions such as "What are five areas of concern for parents and children in blended families?" "What are your needs?" "Where does it hurt?" "What has been most helpful for your situation?" and "What is one thing about the blended family experience that no one ever talks about and that you need to talk about?" "How has Christian faith helped you?" We brainstormed and were able to craft a course that had the Bible as its foundation and human experience as its structure.

● *Adults are oriented to their tasks, roles, and identity.* This means that the learner's identity — as parent, spouse, worker, professional, or recreational hobbyist — profoundly affects what the learner is willing to learn about. Good adult education is intimately linked to people's image of themselves and what they see as their role and function in the world.

For example, in our culture women are vitally concerned about their role and function. The woman who has made the decision to be a traditional wife and mother spends a lot of time and energy concerned about those roles, especially if many of her female friends have careers. Then when she completes the bulk of her child-rearing by her middle forties, she's got to figure out what she is supposed to do for the next thirty-five years. What are the resources of faith for her?

An effective adult education program will integrate such concerns about roles with biblical curriculum.

● *Adults want knowledge that can be immediately applied.* Probably no more than 10 percent of adults are genuinely interested in learning for learning's sake, to know the Bible simply in order to know the Bible, to know theology or church history or Christian philosophy simply because they enjoy learning. Unlike many children and youth, adults are unwilling to store up theoretical knowledge that may or may not someday be of use to them.

For most adults, the someday of their childhood has arrived, and they want to see the practical benefits of learning today. They want information they can use now. They want connections to everyday life. So it's harder to "market" a course on the doctrinal themes in Hebrews than a course on parenting teenagers. This doesn't mean you avoid Hebrews, but you must connect it to questions they're asking.

Often then, I look for teachable moments in adult lives, windows of opportunity when a course subject matches the felt need of the learner.

For example, I frequently conduct a class called "Teaching

Values to Children," and I've found that the time parents are most open to this course is within the first few months after a baby is born. Two years later, they feel they already know how to parent. They've settled into patterns. But later still, when their children move into new and more challenging phases, new teachable moments will occur.

So one of our jobs is to catch people at those transition points in their lives, when they are trying on new roles, exploring new situations, facing new challenges.

That's not to say that adult needs should rule the classroom. Although I recognize the need to touch adults at their points of needs, most of my teaching is essentially Bible-centered. But I always try to find those crucial links between the Bible and real-world living.

Teaching that Connects with Adults

While keeping in mind the characteristics of adult learners, I structure my teaching so that it connects with adults. For me, there are at least six keys.

1. Treat adults as adults. This obvious point is, unfortunately, sometimes overlooked.

In one church where I was working with the adult education program, a teacher whose class was practically evaporating before her eyes came to me in a panic.

"I need you to come observe my class," she said. "I only have a few people left. Please tell me what I'm doing wrong before my class disappears completely!"

So I visited her class, and in the first minute or so I knew exactly what was wrong.

"Now, class," she said in a voice more patronizing than a schoolmarm addressing a roomful of second-graders, "let's open our Bibles and turn to John chapter 3. That's the Gospel of John, not the epistles. If you have one of the pew Bibles I set out on the back table, you'll find it on page 927. Just run your finger down the margin and find verse 16. Does everyone have the verse now?" Her manner was like a fingernail on a chalkboard. No wonder her class was evaporating!

Yet there's more to treating adults like adults than the voice or teaching style. The room itself must respect their sensibilities.

Unfortunately, many church classrooms smell like church classrooms: old, stale, and flat. Although we in the church get used to that smell, that can subtly bother people who are new to our fellowship.

By "smell," I mean more than olfactory sensation. Churches also have a visual "smell." A lot of churches — particularly smaller, older churches — consign their adult education classes to a dungeon-like basement with cracked linoleum floors, cold, hard folding chairs, and children's Sunday school posters from the sixties.

One reason many new, large megachurches are so inviting to adults is that they don't have this church "smell." They have windows, sunlight, fresh air, clean bathrooms, fresh paint, attractive visuals, comfortable chairs — in short, all the signs of a place that is alive and open.

As we look at our own churches, we should ask ourselves, "Is this a place where adults would enjoy gathering and spending time together? Does it look clean? Are the chairs comfortable? Can people hear? Are the aesthetics pleasing to adult sensibilities?"

Another consideration: Do we put visitors on the spot? Do we make them feel awkward and conspicuous? People and church cultures vary, but the older I've gotten the less I'm willing to enter a new situation only to be told to stand up and talk about myself. And if I'm made to feel uncomfortable in a given social climate, I tend to avoid it thereafter.

2. *Diagnose needs.* I am constantly in the process of examining where my people are and what they need. There are three primary ways I do that.

● Interviews. I've had Christian education committees conduct interviews with adults in the congregation. Surveys can be helpful too, but one-on-one or two-on-one interviews reap wonderful results for adult education.

I suggest that people from various categories be interviewed:

young married couples, couples married less than three years, long-time members, widowed, never married, single parents, parents of adolescents, businesspeople, working women, housewives, the divorced — the exact categories depend, of course, on the composition of the congregation.

Then the pastor and/or members of the adult education committee have a conversation with individuals or couples, asking questions such as:

— In the last two years, have you undergone a transition, change, or crisis? How might the church have helped you to cope and grow during that time?

— What stage are you at in your spiritual pilgrimage? Beginner? Stumbling along? Mature? How do you feel about where you are? How can the church help you grow as a Christian?

— What are some needs your acquaintances have that the church could address? How could we equip you to meet them?

When the answers are gathered, they shed a great deal of light on how to best teach adults so that their needs are addressed.

● Pretests. Another way to diagnose needs is with a pretest. The first Sunday of a new series, I often give a little test — brief and easy to complete — that lets me know the general level of biblical understanding in the group. For example, I might give the class a five-minute quiz, asking them to define four key words from Romans. This tells me how well they understand concepts like "grace" and "salvation" and whether I need to do factual teaching or can move on to wrestle with application.

Sometimes I've passed out the three-by-five cards at intervals throughout the class to check in. I'll ask, "What's the most important thing you've learned so far?" or "What's the biggest question you have about Romans still?" That feedback helps me keep my finger on the learner's pulse so that I can make mid-course corrections.

● Observation. By staying alert in class, I can gain a number of insights into people by simply watching them.

I notice, for instance, how people enter the classroom. If I see that two sit on the third row on the right, and then two on the fifth row on the left, and then one on the inside aisle up front, and then a few on the back row — I'm probably dealing with people who don't know each other or don't feel comfortable with one another.

If people come and sit in groups, one group to the left, another to the right, it may indicate a certain cliquishness. If people come in and speak quietly but politely to one another, it may indicate they don't know each other well. If people come in boisterous, gently ribbing one another, it may indicate I'm teaching people who know each other well.

Too often we only look at the size of the class after it's full. At that point, it looks like a community because every chair is full. But when I notice how those chairs were filled, I learn a lot about my class.

3. Involve the learners in planning their own learning. The most effective courses always begin this way.

Several years ago, I was preparing to teach a course on women in transition. Although I had taught this subject a number of times and considered myself an "expert," I decided to involve the learners in the planning process. I'm glad I did.

When I gathered a group of women to brainstorm on this subject, I asked them questions like, "What transitions do you think women are experiencing? What do you think are some of the hardest issues faced by women in transition?" They were reeling off answers I had heard before, but then one woman surprised me.

"If the class meets on Sunday nights," she said, "I need to get my husband's permission to come." It had never occurred to me that these women would feel they needed permission to participate in a church activity. Together we began exploring this issue of husband/wife decision making, and we designed a class that would address the many issues surrounding it.

I had originally planned the class for twenty women, but by the time the planning was through, and word had gotten around, 110 women had signed up. Planning with people helps them stay in control of the learning process, helping them address their concerns.

4. Make adults responsible for their learning. I avoid coaxing adults into learning because doing so treats them like children. Instead, I make them responsible for the learning they want to do. I do that sometimes by asking them to make a learning commitment or contract.

I might begin a class in the Book of John by saying, "There are three levels at which you can take this class: Level One: You can come and receive whatever is presented. Just be willing to enter into the discussion.

"Level Two: As you take this class, you will read William Barclay's commentary on John.

"Level Three: Bring a notebook and plan to do your daily devotions and meditations in John. You may even want to do your family devotions in this book."

Then I hand out a simple questionnaire and ask people to make a commitment.

This way I get a sense of the overall character of the class. Sometimes I find I have a class full of people who just want to sit and absorb, so I structure the curriculum to meet their needs. Other times I may have seven people who want to work with the commentary, four who are linking the class to their daily devotions, and one who actually wants to put out a graduate-level effort. It's extremely helpful to know your audience.

I once taught a class on Romans in which the highest commitment level group was given the name "The Royal Fork Club." It was named after The Royal Fork, an inexpensive buffet restaurant. I told the class I would pick up the tab for a buffet dinner for those in The Royal Fork Club who completed all the exercises week by week. I figured that at most five or six people would sign the contract.

Instead, we had over a hundred sign up! Since this idea proved too successful for my own financial well-being, we had to find a donor to sponsor The Royal Fork Club.

5. Help adults see learning as a lifelong endeavor. One of my goals is to encourage a lifelong love and fascination for the subject I teach. The learner should not be able to say at the conclusion of a course on

Exodus, "Well, now I have that subject behind me." He should want to continue studying the subject after the class is over. If I teach Exodus in such a way that people say, "I've done Exodus; I'm glad I don't ever need to study Exodus again," then I've failed. I have not ignited the flame of curiosity and fascination in that learner.

One way to inspire a continuing interest in the subject is to provide the right kind of closure at the end of the course. The class should not just stop. It should reach an emotionally satisfying conclusion yet suggest that there is more to learn.

Guided reflection on the learning process is one way I've brought a class such closure. I ask, "What's the most important thing you've learned in this course? What is one thing you've learned that you intend to put into practice in your everyday life? What is one issue arising from this course that you still don't understand, that you still want to study further, or that you still need to work on in order to apply to your life?" They either respond verbally in small groups or write out answers on paper.

In this way, I've communicated clearly that we haven't learned everything there is to know about the subject, yet I've helped them see what they've learned and what difference it will make. The learning process hasn't ended with this course. It has just been launched.

I recently received a letter from a former student saying, "I'm re-listening to tapes of your courses in Romans and Exodus. In fact, this is my fourth time in over five years that I've listened to them. Each time, I'm at a different level of understanding and a different place in my walk with the Lord. I've learned something new at each level."

This, to me, is what adult Christian education is about. It's a dynamic, interactive process where both teacher and learners have a meaningful and ongoing relationship with each other and with biblical truth. We share a journey together, and we each come away not just better informed but truly changed.

When I can help my congregation make discoveries just a split second before I actually tell them, they get excited about the Scripture and its relevance for their lives.

— Earl Palmer

CHAPTER EIGHT

Teaching through Preaching

Whenever I stand before a congregation, I have to suppress my natural instinct to preach. We preachers have a tendency — some innate drive — to offer answers to our listeners before they've even heard the questions. We want to help, but sometimes we forget the process required.

No wonder preaching has gotten a bad name. "Don't preach at me!" a teenager shouts at his parents. "I don't need your sermon," a wife says to her husband. And we know exactly what they mean. People resist answers others have found for them. Now-I'm-going-to-fix-you sermons make my congregation's eyes glaze over. When I pontificate, they cannot contemplate.

J. B. Phillips, while translating the New Testament, discovered its truth to be pulsing with life and power. He felt like an electrician, he said, working with wiring while the power was still on. Grappling with the dynamic, living Word was no dull routine! Phillips felt the awesomeness — both the dread and the excitement — of the electric charge of God's truth.

I've found over the years that I cannot merely preach if I want to convey the power in God's Word. If I want my listeners to know the electricity of living truth, I must somehow bring people to touch personally the power surging through the gospel. I have, then, always tried to make sure my preaching is really teaching, not so much telling people what the truth is as helping them discover truth for themselves.

Teaching: Risking Discovery

Historically, the church has preferred highly controlled teaching, often choosing the seemingly safe methods of instruction. A catechism, for example, sets up a limited number of predetermined questions to be answered. It's a weak teaching device, however, because it does not help people discover the source of the answers it gives. Consequently, they don't necessarily encounter the life of Christ in the catechism.

I don't want to discredit the value of such methods, but they can't substitute for a journey of personal discovery in the Scripture. When I use a catechism, a hymn, or someone's witness, I do not call that teaching. I call it an affirmation. Affirmations reinforce the truth, but they do not teach; they do not help people discover truth for themselves, the essence of good teaching.

Helping people discover truth entails some risks, because we lose some measure of control. We put truth in the hands of others and have to let go; we have to trust that they will personally discover its relevance. But what if they get into spiritual difficulties? What if they stray from orthodox interpretations?

Yet, I've found I need to take those risks and relinquish rigid control of the text. I've learned to trust the Bible to be its own protection against misinterpretation rather than rush in too quickly myself to protect it.

C. S. Lewis was a master at letting the truth of the gospel weave its way into people's lives, giving people room to discover its truth. A man who had liked his *Screwtape Letters* went on to read *Mere Christianity*, and he was infuriated. He wrote Lewis a scathing letter.

"I'm not surprised," Lewis wrote back, "that a man who agreed with me in *Screwtape* . . . might disagree with me when I wrote about religion. We can hardly discuss the whole matter by post, can we? I'll only make one shot. When people object, as you do, that if Jesus was God as well as man, then he had an unfair advantage which deprives him for them of all value, it seems to me as if a man struggling in the water should refuse a rope thrown to him by another who had one foot on the bank, saying 'Oh you have an unfair advantage.' It is because of that advantage that he can help.

"But all good wishes. We must just differ; in charity I hope. You must not be angry with me for believing, you know; I'm not angry with you."

Lewis responds by giving him but one thing to think about, and then he steps back. He puts the matter in the man's hands, as if to say, "Your move." He lets the man now continue the journey of discovery.

Although this can be risky, especially when you're dealing directly with the Bible, I've found the risk small. Our congregation's Bible study groups aren't under particularly close staff supervision; we don't have time to monitor what's going on in every group. Nonetheless, there have been very few instances where the groups have wandered into the nonbiblical or cultic edges. I believe that's because the Bible, when it is read sentence by sentence, draws us toward its living center, which is Jesus Christ.

Instead of spoon-feeding truth to the people, then, I have to want to risk giving them the spoon, letting them discover the satisfying taste of the gospel.

Keep the Bible First

Once while traveling, my daughter and I heard a sermon on the radio. The preacher read the text magnificently; it was from Romans 8 and was about hope. The preacher then gave a series of moving, personal anecdotes about hope.

After the sermon my daughter asked, "How did you like the sermon?"

"It was moving," I said. "In fact, one of the illustrations brought me to tears."

Then my daughter said something I'll never forget: "But Dad, I didn't like the sermon because the pastor basically said, 'Since I have hope, you should have hope.' And that's not gospel."

I was so proud of my daughter. She saw that the Good News was something more. I'm glad this pastor has hope. But I need to see how that text in Romans gives me a profound basis for hope whether he has hope or not! In a way then, the pastor cheated his listeners. We were denied the opportunity to see the text and discover from it the basis of hope for ourselves.

People, of course, desire a human touch — love and compassion and hope. And they need personal stories to show the gospel in action in daily life. The only trouble is, personal stories alone don't connect me to the real source of hope.

Personal witness and stories should be seen like all illustrations — as windows to illuminate, to help people look in on a textual treasure waiting to be discovered. If I make my discoveries through such stories, I may become unhealthily dependent on the story teller, usually the pastor, for my spiritual growth. But if I can discover hope for myself from Romans 8, I discover it alongside the pastor. Although it takes more time, this discovery is more powerful and long lasting.

Yes, we must be people fluent, understanding them and communicating to their needs. But first we must be textually fluent. That means, of course, I must invest time and hard work to know the text. In fact, I have to know a lot just to raise the right questions! Good teaching comes when I understand the content and deeply know the text before I search for its implications. Then people can be connected first and foremost with the text.

Let the Urgency Come Through

Letting the Scripture speak for itself doesn't mean I'm dispassionate about my presentation. If I want my learners to discover the text, I need to whet their appetite for spiritual things. To do that effectively I need to convey the urgency of the text.

The best calculus teachers believe a kid can't really make it in the world without knowing calculus. The best school teachers are convinced their courses are the most important ones offered. Such teachers demand more and challenge more. They also teach more.

I want to capture a sense of urgency that says, "This is not just an interesting option. It is essential that you know." Learners catch more than content from such teaching; they catch an enthusiasm for the truth. Excited teachers make learning urgent; bored teachers make it a task.

This means, among other things, I must be urgent about my own soul. I must be a growing, maturing Christian myself with an appetite for spiritual things. Only then can I communicate with urgency the need for my congregation to grow and mature as well.

Don't Get to the Point

Although I'm urgent about what I teach, I'm not urgent about getting to the main point of the text. I've learned not to reveal what I know too soon. I've learned not to force the discovery, but to let the natural drift of the text unfold. I've got to give people time to wonder, time to ponder, time for questions to emerge, and time for answers to take shape in the text.

When I preach by raising questions that spring naturally from the text itself, I enable the listener to discover meaning for themselves. It's a little like Agatha Christie holding the solution to the mystery until the time is just right.

Take, for example, the text about Zacchaeus in Luke 19:1-11. After Zacchaeus received Jesus into his home, the next line says, "They all murmured, 'He is gone to be the guest of a man who is a sinner.' " Even though I want to highlight this detail quickly, I don't need to tell the congregation right off why the people murmured.

So first I'll ask them, "Why did the people murmur? Why are they so upset? What's going on that they're so angry with Jesus? And notice, they *all* murmured — that means the disciples, too. Why are the disciples upset?"

I may journey with my congregation through the various kinds of people who'd have been present in Jericho: Why would the Pharisees murmur? Why the disciples? Why the townspeople? What upsets them so? What expectations did they have that Jesus now has dashed?

Such an approach retains the text's natural drama.

With this particular story, I can take my congregation on a journey through some Old Testament expectations of the Messiah. I can explore various ideas of what the Messiah would and wouldn't do with a crook like Zacchaeus. I can consider why people weren't prepared for a Messiah who came to seek and to save the lost. I can show why they were so surprised by Jesus.

It's this surprise element in the text that is the wonderful good news! When I can help my congregation make such discoveries just a split second before I actually tell them, they get excited about the Scripture and its relevance for their lives.

Let the Truth Sell Itself

We teachers are often tempted to say too much all at once, especially at the end of lessons and sermons. We throw in everything we can think of to make someone a Christian, rattling off the most precious facts of our faith — the blood of Christ, the cross, God's love — and reduce them to hasty, unexplained sentences.

Instead, I've found it is far better to let the scriptural text make its own point and sell itself. And we can trust Scripture to make its own point because the Spirit is already working in people before they even come to the text.

I see this in culture: Woody Allen movies, among other examples, may not be Christian, but they force people to grapple with ultimate issues, which is where God most often is found. I also see the Spirit working in people's lives: they struggle with grief and worry and meaning in life.

People come to the text not as blank slates but as individuals in whom the Spirit is already working. Since the Scripture speaks to people's deepest needs, we can trust that it will get a hearing. We can be confident people also will discover how good it is once they give it a try.

It's like taking a friend to Mount Hood: I've been to Timberline Lodge and I know how beautiful it is. But I don't have to brag about it beforehand to convince my friend of its magnificence. All I have to do is get him there, and he'll see its impressive beauty for himself.

All I have to do is bring people to the door of Scripture. Once they walk through and see for themselves, they're going to be struck with how relevant Jesus Christ is for their lives.

In our church's small group Bible studies, for instance, we don't try to be evangelistic. Our goal is to let the text make its own point and then enable the group to talk together about what is being read. We consciously try not to cover everything the first week but only what the text for the first week says.

Our approach is this: "Read this book like you read anything else. When you start into Mark, don't give him an inch; make him win every point. Don't worry about whether this is supposed to be the holy Word of God or not; just read it with the same seriousness you apply to your own thoughts."

The amazing thing is that the text inevitably reveals its living center, Jesus Christ. Some weeks Mark (or Paul or John) wins, convincing people of some truth. Frankly, some weeks he loses: people leave thinking they know better than Mark. But over time, the text comes out ahead, and the Christ of the text wins respect — and the heart of a new believer.

A crusty engineering professor in our city was shattered when his wife died of a sudden heart attack, and just before he was to retire. She had been a Christian, and after the funeral, he came to see me. I steered him toward the Gospel of Mark and some additional reading.

After several weeks, I could see the New Testament was gradually making sense to him. My closing comment in our times together was usually, "Let me know when you're ready to become a Christian."

One Sunday after church, with a lot of people milling around, the engineer stood in the back waiting for me. He's not the kind of man who likes standing around. Finally he got my attention, and he called out, "Hey Earl, I'm letting you know."

That was it. He became a Christian at age 65, convinced by the Scripture of Christ's trustworthiness.

Letting People Hear Their Own Application

Creating opportunity for personal discovery sometimes surprises us in the way results come. One pastor struggled with the way his conservative upbringing imposed artificial spirituality on people. He refused to preach on traditional "sins": going to movies, smoking, drinking, and so on.

One Sunday his text gave him ample opportunity to talk of such things: "All things are lawful, but I will not be mastered by anything." However the pastor still would not mention the sins dictated by his tradition. Instead, he deliberately spoke of other addictions tolerated by his church, things such as overeating and watching too much television.

After the service one woman cornered the pastor, handing him her pack of cigarettes. "It may be lawful," she said, "but I've been mastered by these cigarettes. I've never noticed that verse in that way before, so I'm giving these to you. With God's help, I'm going to master them." Without a word about cigarettes or nicotine, the text itself had spoken to this young woman.

That pastor could have preached against her cigarettes and maybe even have convinced her to quit smoking. But when the pastor does the work of connecting the text so specifically to life, such a decision is not as likely to stick.

Instead, she herself made the connection between the text and her smoking. And I have found that change goes deeper when *we* make the connection, when *we* discover God's Word to us.

When I can help people discover that, then I'm "teaching" a great deal and preaching as I should.

PART THREE

The Longer View

Experience in teaching doesn't tend to sharpen my abilities; rather it dulls them. It is evaluated experience that improves my skills.

— Howard Hendricks

CHAPTER NINE

How Do You Know You're Effective?

Most people think experience is the name of the game, that the longer a person teaches, the better he or she gets. Nonsense. Just as ripping through wood dulls the teeth of a carpenter's saw, so experience tends to wear away my edge. I have found only *evaluated* experience sharpens my skills. Evaluation hones the edge.

Teaching without evaluation can erode my effectiveness in many ways. Poor methods become ingrained habits. I can assume I'm doing better than I really am and become complacent. I can conclude something works when it actually doesn't. I can lose touch with my audience, teaching in a vacuum. Also, time exaggerates my idiosyncrasies rather than lessening them. And without anything to keep me on my toes, I can get sloppy.

That's why, like the carpenter who painstakingly files each tooth on his crosscut saw, I evaluate every session I teach. And I invite others to critique me in various ways. The longer I go, the more I feel the need. But I find that many pastors and teachers have serious reservations about evaluation.

Overcoming Our Hesitancy

Some may fear evaluation undermines their authority: "If I encourage people to take a critical look at me, they will take it on as their role in life. I'm opening Pandora's box. They will assume I'm more interested in their opinions and preferences than God's. It may suggest that I'm merely giving a performance. Would Jeremiah ask the Jews to evaluate his prophecy?"

I have found, however, that inviting evaluation has precisely the opposite effect. A teacher who is vulnerable, realistic, and committed to excellence wins the respect of others. It shows personal security and strength. Especially in our society, pedestals diminish credibility, while leaders who are open with others gain respect.

Inviting evaluation also helps people identify with me and become more supportive of my ministry; in a sense I'm recruiting them on my team. I will often ask the conference director of the event I'm speaking at to evaluate my messages, both before and after giving them. That not only helps me hone my skills, it reinforces the idea that together we're trying to make for an effective conference.

Second, some may hesitate to invite evaluation because of other people's biases. One person wants us to exegete the Bible verse by verse. Another wants a string of stories. One wants us to shout; another wants us to quiet down. One says we're too emotional, another that we need more urgency. One wants us to speak more to human needs, while another decries our lack of doctrinal content.

Each one wants us to imitate his or her favorite preacher.

Although people think it is a matter of right or wrong, we know it is a matter of preference or style or gifts, and so we don't think they are qualified to comment.

People may indeed be biased, but I still don't want to jettison evaluation. I have found that I simply must evaluate the evaluations. I have to recognize where people are coming from and read their comments with that perspective.

On one occasion I received a cryptic note from a woman who felt my sense of humor was unspiritual. In fact, she threatened to get up and walk out, with her companions, if I continued to "indulge in levity." I double-checked with the coordinator of the event at which I was speaking and with his full support went on as usual. Nobody got up and walked out, but I was better informed about my audience.

The greater the number of evaluators, though, the more I will get a balanced profile of my own ministry. I will recognize the extremes on both ends. Even the extremes can help me see that, yes, I could use a little humor, for example, or more stories. Even fierce critics can be my best friends.

For better or worse, I don't teach in a vacuum. I cannot disregard how people perceive me, for they are my "customers." Even if professional rhetoricians and homileticians reviewed my every message approvingly, in the end my most important evaluators are still the people who receive my ministry. If they're not sensing the benefit, something has to change.

Third, some of us can fear the truth. We may not be ready to face up to the fact that our teaching has failings. We avoid evaluations like any bad news. But I have found that bad news catches up with me sooner or later, and much more painfully than if I had faced it while I could do something about it.

For example, in the past I have used illustrations from my family that they did not heartily appreciate. Also, in my early years I sometimes used big words in my teaching. Before long some friends who were honest and secure enough confronted me head-on with my lack of judgment, and I corrected myself. I appreciate them for it.

Fourth, we can overspiritualize the issue: "It's not my job, or anybody else's, to grade my ministry. Only God can judge that. In teaching, unseen things happen that won't be known till judgment day."

As true as that is, I've still found that the Holy Spirit who helps me understand the Bible and prepare my messages also teaches me through others how to do it more effectively. He may be the source of wisdom for me, yet he helps communicate that wisdom through others. Perceptive listeners who ask questions are probably my best source for improvement. I know from them what I left out, what I skimmed over too quickly, perhaps even what I had not thought through well enough.

Finally, we recognize how difficult it is to evaluate the intangibles of ministry. Other vocations have objective ways of determining whether a person is getting the job done. If 60 percent of a surgeon's patients are dying, it's clear he's got a problem. A lawyer either wins the case or loses. We can see whether a carpenter has plumbed his building square.

But how do we quantify spirituality? When people sin and fail, can we take the blame for a fallen culture? What if we are doing the hard work of sowing while a more fortunate worker reaps? Lacking objective measures, people end up looking at the externals: buildings, money, baptisms, programs. Faced with such superficiality, we may say "No thanks" to evaluations.

This is a false dilemma, however. I've found valid criteria for determining whether my teaching is well communicated and well delivered, and whether people are finding helpful truth for their lives.

What I Evaluate

Though we can never be as exact as a scientist, we can realistically evaluate the effectiveness of teaching by asking two broad questions.

• *Am I reaching my ultimate goal?* I have set a twofold goal: (1) to present believers perfect in Christ, as Paul describes in Colossians 1:28 and 29, and (2) to equip them for ministry, according to Ephesians 4:15 and 16. Therefore my objective as a teacher is definitely not the mere passing along of information; it is nothing less than change and maturation.

I can assess that by looking at the lives of those I teach. But the number one question I ask is not "Where are they?" but "In what direction are they moving?" I find that out by getting alongside people, talking with them, finding out how they're implementing these nuggets I'm handing out.

A pharmacist and his wife trusted Christ and enrolled in my course on the Christian home. After only a few sessions they came to me and said, "We never knew we had a problem until we started to study the Scripture. We thought all marriages were as troubled as ours." My wife and I stayed in touch with this couple as they began to deal with new insights. Not only did their marriage improve, they also saw radical changes in their children. Meanwhile I saw that the gospel I taught was clearly life-changing.

Often, however, the effects of our teaching won't be fully seen until a crisis. One of my students, for example, may not show a lot of outward change in her conduct, but when her father or mother dies suddenly, and she works through her grief with a strong trust in God, dedicating herself even more deeply to serve the Lord, I know that the seeds I planted have taken root. Nothing reveals what's growing under the soil like a spiritual test. So that's another time I can evaluate the effectiveness of my teaching.

I also try to note the class's immediate reaction to my teaching. I'm suspicious of my teaching if people just pack their belongings and walk out of the room when class ends. I know I've done something right when students "whoosh" to the front and besiege me with questions.

Effective teaching has to provoke something, unsettle some cherished notions, open people's eyes to things they've never realized. Effective truth is a catalyst in the minds and emotions, causing a spiritual reaction. If I'm doing my job — provoking people to think about things in a way they never have — I'll hear about it.

I also watch keenly for a change in values. Ultimately that's where all change begins. After a recent teaching series, a man in our church said to me, "I don't know where I've been all my life. I can't believe I could be that far removed from the real target."

"What do you think the real target is?" I asked.

"Well, I've suddenly realized my family is my greatest asset. I've been selling my soul for a mess of pottage."

Even if I can't follow that man around and see whether he's spending more time with his family, I know his values have shifted.

I also look for other key attitudes, especially an increasing hunger for God and his righteousness. Are people starting to fall in love with the Lord? Is there some evidence of the supernatural in their lives? Are people being delivered from self? Are they starting to care about others?

● *Does my teaching communicate?* That's not hard to evaluate. For one thing, if I don't have enough illustrations to bring light into my material, it will fall short. So I can look at my notes and count the number of illustrations.

I can also look at the number of stories I tell. Narratives improve communication. Whether stories come from the Bible, my personal experience, the newspaper, or other people, I know that my people won't identify as well with my messages without them.

Dale Carnegie discovered this right from the start. When he began in New York, he had twenty-seven or so people in his first class. The students were only required to pay him a week at a time, so if they didn't enjoy it, they wouldn't come back. He knew if he didn't connect, he was finished.

In his first class, he ran out of material before the hour was up. In a panic he called a fellow from the front row to come to the front of the class, and he started asking him questions about his life. The guy talked, and the class was interested. He learned that people are interested in people and people's stories.

I also evaluate the quantity of material I cover. My anthropology teacher at Wheaton College was one of the finest teachers I've had. One time I asked the teacher, "Doctor, how do you do it?"

"I take the material," he said, "boil it down to the irreducible minimum, and then spread it over the semester."

I think about that when I hear messages that have so much information in them that listeners can't possibly assimilate it all. That's like trying to give someone a drink with an open fire hydrant. When I do that, I may be dispensing information, but I'm not being effective.

I also evaluate my transitions. I don't want to fall into the trap of planning what to say but not how to say it: "Now, I want to illustrate this point, because it's a very important point, and I was reading in the Bible the other day, and I came across an illustration out of the life of Elijah, and it was a real grabber, and I want you to see it, 'cause it'll drive home the point."

In all that piffle I haven't said anything, but I've consumed a lot of time. So I objectively evaluate whether I've pinpointed my transitions: "One morning Elijah's servant awoke him early . . ."

How I Evaluate

A chef in pursuit of culinary perfection wants feedback from more than one gourmet or one customer. Likewise the more people who critique my teaching, the more evaluation methods used, the more likely I will gain an accurate and thorough picture of my effectiveness.

To begin with, then, I evaluate myself briefly after every teaching opportunity, and I ask three questions.

1. What did I do well? If I only highlight failings, my confidence suffers. I need to encourage myself with the positive, for by affirming the good I reinforce it.

2. What did I do poorly? During my teaching I will sense when I don't connect or communicate clearly. Often the best time to pinpoint the cause is immediately afterward.

3. What should I change? Sometimes, for instance, I will decide afterward to convert what I've just taught into handouts. Or I may have discovered a type of illustration or story that resonates, so I'll plan more of the same for the future. I also make specific, step-by-step plans to fill any gaps.

This only scratches the surface of the self-evaluation I do.

Together with my wife I evaluate my life and ministry daily as well as doing periodic check-ups on a broader scale. For many years, especially when our young family tended to distract, Jeanne and I scheduled occasional weekends for planning and praying together. We tried to put the past, present, and future into perspective. Nothing in our marriage has been more effective for gaining a sense of direction.

I also invite others to evaluate my teaching both in writing and verbally. Since most people don't like saying anything negative to my face, I often use written evaluations. This also helps them give a careful assessment. Verbal feedback, though, is useful sometimes: it's immediate; comments can be clarified; I can read the person's body language and so "hear" more nuances in their remarks.

How I frame questions significantly affects the feedback. I ask open-ended questions ("What parts of this class helped you?") that harvest whatever is on the evaluator's mind, or directive questions ("Did my introduction get your attention?") to point them specifically to issues I'm curious about.

Periodically I debrief a class. I sit down with some students over refreshments and ask what spoke to them, what they understood me to be saying, what questions they have. I've found this one of the more productive means of feedback.

On occasion I will gather a focus group that represents various demographic slices in my church. It might include young singles, married couples with teens, or retirees. Not long ago my wife and I met with some senior citizens in a retirement center. We wanted to hear their thinking, their problems, their dreams in order to devise ministry that meets specific needs.

In addition, I've been helped by bringing in a professional —a college speech professor, for example. He will spot things that the untrained eye would overlook, offering a sophisticated critique of the finer points of teaching.

There is a cost to evaluation, as well as a payoff. It requires time, effort, and openness. On some days it encourages me; on others, it knocks the wind out. Frequently evaluation turns up nothing new. But then come those precious, few insights that advance my effectiveness by a quantum leap.

Finally, I keep one thought in mind as I consider my evaluations: I'm never quite as bad as I, or others, think. Nor am I quite as good. Because of evaluation, though, I am improving.

Recruiting is a ministry of discernment. It is the holy act of helping others discover their gifts and discern God's will.

— Roberta Hestenes

CHAPTER TEN
Recruiting and Keeping Teachers

Some years ago I was responsible for recruiting someone to oversee a pastoral care program involving over two hundred adults. It was a big job, and I was looking for a couple who could commit a great deal of time and energy to the program.

I prayed about this problem literally for months, wondering who would be willing and able to take on such a challenge. Eventually I sensed the Lord pointing me to Bill and Terri, a couple in their late thirties. I stopped them in the hall at church one Wednesday evening and said, "I have a new opportunity for ministry in mind for you. Would you be willing to meet and discuss it?"

The following week, they and I sat down together in my living room, and I laid out my proposal. I spelled out the importance of the program to the life of the church and told them all the reasons I felt they were the right couple for this ministry.

"I'm not going to sugarcoat this job," I added. "It's going to be tough." And I carefully sketched in all the downsides I could think of. The church staff was already stretched too thin, so they wouldn't get much in the way of help or additional resources. The hours would be long, and the job largely thankless. Yet the opportunity was significant.

I was beginning to think I had oversold the downside when Bill and Terri looked each other and then at me and grinned.

"In the car on the way over here," Bill said, "we were wondering what sort of job you had in mind. And we said to ourselves, 'If this is another one of those Mickey Mouse church jobs, we don't want it.' But you've given us something that really counts! We'll do it."

"Well, wait a minute!" I cautioned. "Don't say yes so fast! Pray about it, think about, then get back to me."

"All right," said Terri, "we'll pray about it — but the answer will still be yes!"

And it was. In fact, this couple invested a total of fourteen years in that position, and the program was enormously successful under their leadership.

That to me is the prototype of recruiting, and it's the type of conversation and long-term success I want to have when recruiting workers for the educational ministries of the church.

It doesn't always end up successfully, of course. Sometimes getting people to teach is tough: too many jobs to fill and not enough people, the recruiting conversation is awkward, people make excuses. And then when you finally recruit someone, they quit early or refuse to sign up again.

There will always be challenges in recruiting. But over the years I've found a number of practices that help make recruiting less of a chore and more of a ministry, and a successful one at that.

Finding a Ministry, Not Just Doing a Job

People get excited about ministry; they get scared off by jobs. So I don't recruit to jobs; I recruit to ministries, as with Bill and Terri.

Although we are tempted to fall back on "duty" to motivate when recruiting, duty is a very poor motivator compared with the adventure of ministry. People are not inclined to take on jobs for the sake of "duty." But they will take on ministries when they see a chance to make a significant difference in the lives of others.

Consider this recruiting appeal: "I'm asking you to take this teaching job because we need somebody in the classroom every week." Now compare that with this: "We're looking for someone to lay a lasting foundation of faith in the life of young Christians." Which would you find more persuasive?

And it's not just a matter of finding the most persuasive words. I genuinely want to help the potential teacher see how his or her effort in the classroom connects with something larger, with something eternal, with God's plan — but I want to do so with integrity.

That means letting prospective teachers know as precisely as possible what to expect and what's expected of them. I don't hesitate to present the challenges as well as the joys of the assignment I want them to take. After all, if it's a ministry, it will have challenges. But challenges motivate. What de-motivates is a sense of "I'm underemployed. I'm in a Mickey Mouse job."

To a prospective adult teacher, I might say, "You will be responsible to produce a well-written study guide and to spend a minimum of three hours a week preparing for your class. From September to May, this task is demanding. But we have a replacement lined up for you from May through August. You'll be expected to attend teacher training next month, and the leadership conference in May."

Of course, people have different energy levels, different gifts, different lifestyles, different interests, all of which affect how much time and energy they can commit to teaching in the church. In fact, the best way to avoid volunteer burnout is to make sure we challenge a large number of people to share the ministry burden so that the full weight of the work doesn't fall on too few people.

I find, however, that the real problem for most churches is not that people are overworked but that they are underchallenged. So, instead of saying, "Give whatever you can spare," I say, "Give your best to the Lord," asking them to sign on for nothing less than the challenge of ministry through their church.

Recruiting Is Relationships

All recruiting amounts to matching people to needs: you have a class that has certain goals and you find a person who will be able to fulfill those goals.

In order to find a good match, however, the recruiter needs to know the people in the church. It cannot be done in an institutional way. It can only be done in a relational way. We have to know what makes people tick, what gets them excited and enthused, how they enjoy spending their time, and what their passions and motivations are.

For example, let's say I've noticed a young mother who's been attending church for some time. I may be tempted to ask her to babysit in the nursery. But when I get to know her, I discover that she is gifted in relationship skills and has a desire to evangelize. So, instead I might ask her to design a meaningful outreach program for young mothers.

Or let's say there is a lawyer who works with refugees on immigration law. He might be recruited to lead an adult seminar on Christian responses to changing neighborhoods.

The point is we cannot help people find a ministry if we don't know their gifts, abilities, and interests. So good recruiting is an ongoing process of getting to know people at coffee fellowship, at church retreats, in small groups, in Bible studies. As a recruiter of teachers, I believe in visiting people in their homes and at work.

And I believe in using the small-group programs in helping me recruit. If I need a certain kind of teacher for a certain class, I sometimes will call up a small-leader, describe the need, and ask if she knows anyone who can fill the bill. Small groups can be an effective avenue for uncovering and unleashing hidden potential in the church.

The Recruiting Team

I find that the most effective approach to recruiting — particularly in a large church — is a team approach. Hierarchical relationships cannot supply the broad network of relationships, the pool of ideas and imagination, or the depth of mutual support that team relationships provide. Moreover, teamwork — that is, community — is the biblical model for almost all Christian ministry.

A team represents a variety of interests, backgrounds, gifts, and passions. One member of the team has a passion for deep biblical scholarship. Another has a heart for the needs of seniors and retirees. One has a special interest in junior high and high school youth. Another is closely involved with children's ministry.

The best recruiter for a ministry is the person who is closest to that ministry, the person who is the most excited about it. So the person who is enthusiastic about working with second graders is a better recruiter for second grade teachers than even the pastor of the church. With a team approach, individuals can be delegated to contact prospective teachers for the areas where they have the most interest and enthusiasm.

In a comparatively small church — say, 75 to 200 members — the pastor can work closely with the recruiting committee. The pastor knows people and their circumstances, so he or she can submit names to contact and steer the committee away from inappropriate volunteers while protecting confidentiality.

There may be certain classes for which the pastor should be involved in recruiting, such as classes in Bible, theology, or church history. The pastor's request can sometimes be used to inspire teacher participation by underscoring the importance of a certain class. The pastor can convey the overall vision for the class, showing how the course fits into the larger ministry of the church.

But the most important question is "Who has the relationship with the prospective teacher?" In most cases, that's the person who should make the contact. Sometimes the pastor should make the contact. But if a lay member of the recruiting team has a close friendship with a prospective teacher and the pastor only knows that prospective teacher on a casual basis, the lay person should make the contact.

The Recruiting Conversation

A lot of people seem to prefer Sunday mornings as their recruiting time. I think this is a mistake. I don't mind making an initial contact with someone on the church lawn or by the coffee urn, but that is hardly the best place to conduct such an important discussion as a recruiting conversation.

If the stakes are low — say, if I'm recruiting helpers for a banquet next month and I anticipate a friendly answer — then a quick conversation between worship services may be adequate. But if I'm recruiting teachers for a two-year commitment to a class, I don't want to catch someone on the run in the hall on Sunday morning. I don't want to be interrupted at a crucial point by other people. I want a quiet, unhurried environment. A Sunday morning contact should serve only as an invitation to a conversation, not the conversation itself.

I try to schedule recruiting conversations well in advance. For most people, teaching is not just an add on, it's a major rearrangement of their lives. So in April I'm already looking at my needs for September and beyond so I can give prospective teachers the time they need to plan, to pray, and to prioritize.

Ideally, the recruiting conversation should involve sitting down in quiet, comfortable surroundings and sharing the vision, explaining the objectives, spelling out the expectations, and detailing the support you're willing to give. I ask people what they think they will need to do the job. I start thinking through the outline of the course with them, and I ask what books, tapes, or other resources would help them prepare for the class.

"What would you need to function?" I ask. "And what sort of encouragement would you need? For instance, would you like help in recruiting a support team for the class?"

We discuss the "job description" — not a formal written document but an understanding. I believe the recruiting experience should not be a contract negotiation but the creation of a partnership between friends, an informal time of thinking and praying together and reaching a decision. I don't say, "Please respond to the terms on this piece of paper." I say, "Let's seek the will of God together."

I try to recruit people for two-year commitments, with time off during that term so they're not working every week for two solid years. I often tell people, "During the first year, you're learning the job. During the second year, you should be training your successor." Teachers sustain two year-commitments fairly well. Some last much longer, especially if we are careful to schedule breaks, breathers, and vacations.

I try to give the prospective teacher room to sense the authentic guidance of the Holy Spirit. The danger of recruiting is that we can easily become manipulative. We can become so convinced of the rightness and importance of our agenda that we try to bend the will of another person to the needs of our program.

I believe some of the most important time I spend in the recruiting conversation is not the time I spend talking, but the time I spend listening. I listen to the prospective teacher's questions, fears, and apprehensions. I listen for signs of excitement and enthusiasm. And when there is reluctance on the part of the prospective teacher, I listen to discern the difference between reasons and excuses.

Reasons and Excuses

Dealing with excuses is one of the most delicate aspects of recruiting. For one thing, "excuses" are sometimes valid reasons. Learning to tell a reason from an excuse is part of the discernment that goes with recruiting.

If a prospective teacher says to me, "Gee, I'd really love to teach a class, but I'm president of the PTA this year, and I just can't take on another duty right now," my reply would be, "President of the PTA is a strategic position, and I want to support your commitment. Perhaps when your term is up, we can take another look at the possibility of teaching." Then I would stay in touch and show a genuine interest in that person's duties with the PTA.

When people feel your authentic support, you frequently gain a teacher over the long haul. I believe an effective recruiter thinks long term and builds relationships.

If someone just doesn't want to get involved, anything can be an excuse: "My mother comes to town every other weekend" or "Our family likes to go hiking and I just couldn't make a commitment." Those are excuses, pure and simple. If a person really believed the class was worthwhile, such activities would soon take second place.

Confronted with an obvious excuse, I try to discern whether I should take the excuse as a no or change the job description. Sometimes an excuse simply means, "I can't make that big a commitment. If the commitment were smaller, I would consider it." So sometimes I will suggest breaking the job into two or three parts, offering the prospective teacher a portion of the job.

Of course, that doesn't always overcome the excuses. And when I solve the person's "problem" three times, and he or she still thinks of another reason not to do it, I know the person is saying, "I am unwilling, period."

The Inadequacy Excuse

One response that requires some special attention is "the inadequacy excuse," which says, "I don't have the gifts, experience, or knowledge to teach this class."

When you consider it, the inadequacy excuse is actually a good place to begin. People should be intimidated by the job of teaching, whether it is teaching children, youth, or adults. It's a profound responsibility.

No one is adequate. The apostle Paul didn't feel adequate, Moses didn't feel adequate, and I sure don't feel adequate. But we can often answer the inadequacy excuse by offering help, training, prayer support, and resources to the prospective teacher.

One of the most common inadequacy excuses is "I don't know

enough to teach this subject." In that case, I might ask, "Would you feel more confident if I helped you learn the subject?" or "How about if I give you some excellent resources?" or "Would a co-teacher help?" Then I listen carefully to the answers so that I can determine if that person just needs help and encouragement in order to say yes — or if I need to find another teacher.

If after probing, I see that their lack of confidence would hinder their teaching, I try to redirect them to get involved in learning. "Maybe you'll feel better about teaching a class a year from now," I might say, or "Maybe there's another subject you'd be interested in teaching." Many times I have recruited capable, permanent teachers by waiting a year and keeping in touch with them in the meantime.

Naturally, the teacher training offered will make a difference in people's response. If they see that it will answer their concerns and be ongoing, they will more likely have the confidence to say yes to teaching.

Another factor that sometimes elicits "the inadequacy excuse" is the language used when we recruit. I said earlier that I believe in helping the potential teacher see how his or her effort in the classroom connects with something larger, with something eternal, with God's plan. Yet it is possible to overwhelm and intimidate a person by over-stressing the ministry outcome.

If I paint too grandiose a picture of the eternal significance of teaching college students, my prospective teacher is likely to respond, "I'm not a good enough Christian to have that kind of impact!" Instead of inspiring and motivating, I've scared that teacher away!

The language of vision and ministry should be appropriate to the level of the person we're talking to, and appropriate to the level of the teaching task.

Don't Take Yes for an Answer

Another principle I always follow in recruiting: Never let people respond in the initial conversation. My job is not to rope people into my program but to help them discern the will of God.

The question is always, "Is God truly calling you to this ministry?" If God has not called that person, I don't want that person to teach.

So I always close with words to the effect, "Let's pray and think about this possibility for the next few days. Then let's get together a week from now and talk again."

Even if the person says, "Yes, I'll do it," I always say, "I'm glad you feel so positive about it, but would you pray seriously about this? Would you talk it over with your spouse? Then let's get together again and talk."

In this way, I avoid the appearance that I'm simply trying to manipulate people into a position. I also insure that recruits are volunteering after thoughtful and prayerful reflection, so there's a much greater chance that they will stick to their commitment, even through the Elijah Syndrome.

The Elijah Syndrome

Teaching is draining. After a class, many teachers fall into "the Elijah syndrome" — a sense of energy depletion, dissatisfaction, and malaise, often accompanied by spiritual attack in the form of self-doubt and doubting God. We look back on our class time and think, "Who am I kidding? They're not getting anything out of this class. I'm a failure."

I always try to warn new teachers about "the Elijah syndrome," and I suggest ways to counter it. Adult education teachers, for instance, can ask for feedback from their classes. People rarely tell you how the class is affecting them unless you ask. So I suggest that teachers pass out a response card with a few simple questions such as, "What is one thing you learned that has helped your relationship with Christ?" It is encouraging when someone tells you that your teaching made a difference in their life — especially when that person is the quiet one in the back corner who never says a word in class.

Another way to protect teachers against "the Elijah syndrome" is to make sure they have an emotional lifeline securely plugged into the recruiting team. At our church we delegate members of the recruiting team to keep in touch with teachers, asking about their needs, helping them with problems, offering encouragement, and bringing any particularly difficult issues back to the recruiting team for discussion and resolution.

Particularly in the case of new courses or new teachers, I believe in putting a friendly person in the classroom as a support person. This way I can get an independent report on how the class is going, but more importantly, that person can support the teacher by affirming what's going well. It's hard for a teacher to be truly objective about a class, so it's helpful for me and the teacher to draw on an independent viewpoint.

I once had a teacher in an adult education class who always taught to the clock on the back wall; he never looked at his students. So when his class dwindled from fifty to three, he didn't even notice! I would ask him from time to time how his class was going, and he would reply, "Fantastic! I'm really enjoying this class!" For weeks, I took this teacher's report at face value. Then I learned what was happening from one of the few remaining students. That experience confirmed for me the importance of getting friendly but honest independent reports!

Another way to keep in contact with teachers and fend off "the Elijah syndrome" is by sending teachers encouraging notes. I once had a woman on the recruiting team who said, "I can't stand up and teach, but I can write notes to the teachers." That became her ministry. During the middle of the term, when most teachers begin to hit a slump, she sent dozens of handwritten notes sprinkled with honest affirmation, Scripture, and prayer. A number of teachers later told me how those notes gave them a needed lift just as they were slipping into "the Elijah syndrome."

At the end of the term, this woman also wrote thank-you notes to all the teachers. It means a lot when someone comes back just to say, "We genuinely appreciate what you did."

I also believe in rewarding teachers, buying them books or other small gifts, especially gifts that will help prepare them to teach the next class. I gave our Bethel teachers, for example, atlases or Bible handbooks to aid them in their studies. I also like to acknowledge teachers in public by bringing them before the congregation and by printing their names in the bulletin.

Watch Out for De-motivators

Once we have brainstormed our classes into existence, designed them, recruited our gifted and capable teachers, put out our enticing brochures, there is one more thing to watch for. A deadly reef, out of view, hidden beneath the surface, awaits our little boat. It is the reef of de-motivators, details easy to overlook but which can wreak havoc on our educational program. I have seen teachers threaten to quit over de-motivators that could have easily been solved. For example:

• Week after week, an adult education teacher enters the room to find it set up for children. Every Sunday she has to wrestle with furniture in order to create an environment for adults.

• A teacher complains (to no avail) that audio visual equipment doesn't work or isn't available, that the bulbs in the light fixtures are burnt out and never replaced, that there is never any chalk for the blackboard.

• A teacher is discouraged because her class is tucked away in some invisible location in the church, and there are no signs to help people find the room.

I believe it's the teacher's job to teach, and it's the recruiter's job to make sure that the mechanics are taken care of. A teacher should not have to do janitorial and maintenance work in addition to the task of teaching.

Another serious de-motivator arises, particularly in adult education, when the teacher is faced with a class member who has overwhelming emotional or psychological problems. The average teacher just doesn't know what to do in such cases, so the recruiting team must become a backup system to help the teacher deal with those with extraordinary problems.

Teachers should never feel they are dangling at the wrong end of the fishing pole, like a worm waiting for a catfish. Every teacher should have the security of feeling plugged into the larger network. Whenever there's a problem, somebody is ready to find a solution; somebody is available, somebody cares.

What If You Can't Find Anyone to Teach?

During one summer Sunday school session, we couldn't find a teacher for the children's program. People wanted a summer program for their children, yet most of our teachers had left town for the month of August, and we had no volunteers.

Our committee discussed the problem and decided, after some debate, not to hire someone to run the children's program. (I'm not saying it's wrong for a church to do that, but in our situation it wouldn't have worked.) So we put a notice in the church bulletin and announced that there would be no children's classes in August.

This was not an attempt to blackmail people into volunteering. It was simply a solution to the problem, or part of it anyway. In addition, the worship services were altered to be less formal and to better meet the interests of children. Parents took their children with them to worship, and many people thought having the children in the worship service for a few weeks was a benefit rather than a hardship.

Often there is a creative way to solve the problem of no teacher, although it takes flexibility. But before going too far afield, I usually begin by investigating why there are no volunteers. It may be that too many potential teachers are vacationing. It may be that no one wants to be in the 4-year-old room because there is a budding young terrorist in that class.

If the problem simply turns out to be that no one wants to volunteer, then I would probably put an announcement in the bulletin that says, "We have no teacher for this class. If, three weeks from now, we still have no teacher, we will phase out the 4-year-old class." Again, that's not an attempt to manipulate, just telling it like it is.

If there was no response, I would brainstorm with my children's ministry team. Together we would wrestle with the question of why parents or other adults don't feel they have anything at stake in this program, why they feel they should be provided for without any cost to themselves in terms of time and involvement. We would consider recruiting short-term teams to serve one month each, or other creative possibilities. Then, if all else failed, we might merge the 4-year-old class with the 5-year-olds. But we would continue to seek a long-term solution.

The Ministry of Recruiting

There are two passions that motivate people to teach. One is a love for the subject. The other is a love for people. The satisfaction of the recruiting ministry comes from finding people who exhibit this twofold love and from putting their passions to good use. Recruiting is hard work, it's frustrating, it's even painful at times, but it brings great satisfaction to the person who understands the eternal significance of the task.

In the end then, recruiting is a ministry of discernment. It is the holy act of helping others discover their gifts and discern God's will. It begins with prayer; it is facilitated by building relationships. The recruiter's focus is not just on the task but on the person. We are not just running a program; we are building people. We are recruiting for the sake of the teacher as well as for the sake of the church. It's an exciting privilege to be used by God as his instrument to call others into ministry.

If Harvard cannot assume their professors can communicate, how much less can churches.

— *Howard Hendricks*

CHAPTER ELEVEN

Training People to Teach

A young woman, an award-winning interior designer, saw that her church needed a Sunday school teacher for one of the children's classes. She volunteered. They put curriculum in her hands and said, "If you can read it, you can teach it."

She couldn't. She tried, she read, she stumbled through some classes — and she quit. Though it has been years since, she was traumatized by the experience, and if anyone asks her to teach, she responds with a decisive, "No!"

She is not the only gun-shy ex-teacher sitting in the pews of our churches. And who can blame her? At the same time, who can blame pastors, Sunday school superintendents, and education committees? Just as my daughter-in-law had curriculum shoved in her hands, many pastors have teacher training dropped in their laps, having little more expertise in teacher training than she had in teaching. And training teachers can be as tough as teaching a primary class.

But it's not impossible. In fact, multitudes of churches across America — both large and small — are doing an outstanding job of equipping volunteers to teach with excellence. As I have participated in and observed such programs, I see a few common threads that run through their teacher training.

Causing to Learn

First and foremost, effective teachers understand, consciously or intuitively, what teaching is and isn't. Unfortunately, many teachers still think of teaching as dumping content. They assume that when they have unloaded the weekly information from the curriculum, they have taught. As long as they didn't forget what to say or stumble around in the lesson, as long as the students didn't break into bedlam or look too bored, they have succeeded.

But open eyes and a smooth presentation do not measure effective teaching. The ultimate question is not what the teacher does but what the student does as a result of what the teacher does.

Years ago I discovered that the Greek and Hebrew verbs translated in the Bible as "teach" could frequently be translated as "to cause to learn." For example, in classic Greek literature there is a passage where a man picked up a stone and threw it at a tree; then he explained to his son, "This is how you hold the stone. This is how you extend your arm. Keep your eye on the tree and follow through." The father then said, "Now I will see if I have *caused you to learn.*"

This way of looking at teaching revolutionized my approach. Instead of getting worked up about how I was going to tell students what I knew, I began focusing on how I could get them to learn. That made me a much better teacher. So at the beginning of teacher training, I want teachers to see their task in this light.

Building a Database

No one can teach off a blank disk. Teachers need a database from which to draw: Bible facts, doctrines, and teaching principles.

So when we gather, I teach principles of effective teaching, especially *how* students learn. A body-building coach who understands the physics behind muscle development will train better athletes. He understands, for example, that daily weight training on the same muscle groups will tear down muscle fibers without giving them a chance to rest and rebuild.

Likewise, teachers will often fail at causing students to learn unless they know that people learn better when they participate in their learning, when they use what they learn, when they are motivated to learn. *The Seven Laws of Teaching* by John Milton is one book among many that can give teachers guidance in how people learn.

To put teaching in perspective, it's not just any teaching we're doing, but *Christian* education. So I always include some basic doctrine, Old and New Testament introduction, and basic hermeneutics in my teacher training.

The problem, of course, is I don't have time to teach much more than the basics, but effective teachers need continuing enrichment. That's why I teach teachers to study the Bible for themselves. One of the first things I cover when leading a teacher training seminar is inductive Bible study, giving teachers the mental rod and reel to fish for themselves.

Equipping teachers for independent study makes them feel competent, more sure of their teaching, more excited about their work. Bible study and teaching become an adventure of discovering what the Bible teaches. Instead of being completely spoon-fed by me, suddenly they feel free to contribute some of their own insights. We can't teach people everything they need to know, but we can teach them where and how to find it.

How full does the database need to be before you put teachers in a class? When I pastored in Aurora, Illinois, I developed a detailed, eight-month teacher training program. Twenty-seven volunteers faithfully attended the whole course. At the end of those eight months, after they had been sufficiently informed of the basics for teaching Sunday school, I asked for volunteers to teach a class. Of all those thoroughly prepared, eminently qualified people, not a single one volunteered.

They were paralyzed. I had taught them so many things to avoid, so many principles to follow, so many do's and don'ts, they couldn't imagine themselves succeeding in the classroom. The more I had taught them, the more threatening the classroom had become.

Since then I've learned not only to tone down the information I share but intermittently to involve recruits in assisting a mentor before they finish their classroom training.

Mentoring Skills

As important as it is for teachers to have a base of knowledge, it is not enough. While I was Christian education director at a church near Dallas, one teacher walked into my office, tossed his curriculum on the desk, and said, "I'm through."

"What do you mean?" I asked.

"I'm quitting as a teacher."

"Why?"

"Have you been near my class lately? Noise pollution. Kids are climbing the walls. I can't take it anymore."

This man was an engineer, as sharp as a compass point, but apparently he couldn't figure out how to teach fifth graders. So I said, "Well, maybe we have you in the wrong department. What would you think about teaching a different age-level?"

He was too discouraged to say yes, but several weeks later he asked me, "What's that other teaching job you were talking about?"

"We're starting a class for collegians, and we don't have a teacher." After a few days of thought and prayer, he agreed to teach that group, and he was an instant success. He was able to use his usual vocabulary and put his active mind to good use: when critical thinkers challenged him and went for his jugular, he came alive. He enjoyed teaching again, and it was no surprise when I discovered the collegians loved his teaching.

Was this man short on knowledge? No. Did he have the calling and gifts to teach? Absolutely. But he didn't have the skills to discipline and teach young kids. Correcting his problem simply meant either teaching him the skills he needed or moving him to a class he already had the skills to teach.

The point: teachers cannot effectively teach without skills, especially the ability to communicate. Skills buttress confidence, one key to classroom effectiveness. Skills bring enjoyment in a job well done. All in all, skilled teachers are enthusiastic teachers.

Most teachers will be guided by curriculum, but I want them also to know how to organize a lesson, how to illustrate and tell stories, how to be logical, how to deliver a message in a way that sizzles. Just as a chef who knows the science of cooking can make the most out of a book recipe, so a skillful Sunday school teacher can optimize the curriculum.

What is the best way to teach skills? I was talking with the man who heads the training of IBM personnel, and I asked him, "Who's doing the best training? Industry? The military? This is your field. Who do you think is getting the job done?"

"The best training is being done by the cults," he said. "They send people out in twos, with one person always mentoring the other. Once the trainee is capable of going on his own, they say, 'Now you're on the verge of the greatest learning experience of all: taking what we've taught you and teaching it to someone else.' "

Mentoring, of course, is not the invention of the cults. It is the model Jesus gave us, and we are wise to put it to effective use. Here are several things I've done to encourage mentoring of Sunday school teachers:

● *Plant the seed early.* Early in the training process, I tell teachers that I want them eventually to reproduce themselves, to mentor others into teaching. Naturally, beginning teachers are not ready to mentor, but when I announce the goal early, they begin thinking about what helps them teach well and how they might someday help another.

● *Encourage some mutual mentoring.* I want teachers to see themselves as part of a team, in which everyone works together, teachers helping teachers, and people mentoring one another to greater effectiveness. Although I make certain people official mentors, I want people to learn to think of themselves as responsible for others' growth as well as their own — that, after all, is the heart of mentoring.

● *Use the best teachers as trainers.* Mentors will reproduce what they are, whether good or bad. Even if I've had only one good teacher, I've tried to multiply from that one good stock.

I've also put members who are public school teachers to good use. Even though some balk at year-long teaching assignments, many will agree to teach short term, especially if they are asked to act as a mentor to another. They not only feel affirmed for their expertise, they are able to raise the level of the church's teaching ministry.

● *Stagger hands-on involvement.* When it's been possible, I've tried to alternate formal teacher training with experience in the classroom. One week I gather future teachers to train them; the next week I disperse them into classrooms where they observe a trained and experienced teacher, help in the class, and perhaps teach a portion of the lesson. This not only gives people confidence, it makes them more eager learners in the training sessions.

● *Affirm and honor the mentors.* Some people may want to be mentored only by the pastor or Christian education director. But if I regularly affirm and honor the mentors in the department, teachers are more willing to be mentored by them. So I sprinkle generously in training sessions and conversation comments like "John is a marvelous teacher; anyone who is fortunate enough to watch him teach is going to learn something" and "Jennifer has got to be one of the best lesson planners I know."

Igniting Passion

When I visited the Air Force Academy in Colorado some time ago, I talked with the head of the mathematics department. I found out the Air Force has a unique policy about tenure.

"We will not allow a person to teach in the Air Force Academy longer than five years," he said. "After that the teacher must return to active military duty."

"Why is that?" I asked.

"We consider ourselves an infection institution: we want to infect men and women with enthusiasm for the military. We've found that a teacher who is removed from active military service for more than five years is no longer infectious."

Like the military, the church wants teachers who impart not just knowledge and skills but also passion. Without passion there's no life, no drive, no animating energy to the teaching. There's no infectious quality to the message taught. Teachers need more than knowledge and skills to teach effectively. They have to want to teach.

Passion is the most important quality a teacher can have. Those hungry to teach will get knowledge and skills one way or another, whatever price they have to pay. And their passion makes their teaching compelling and winsome. The good news is that there are more people in our congregations with the potential for passion about teaching than we realize.

The Air Force Academy knows what ignites such passion: seeing the difference teaching makes. That's why they put teachers back into active service.

Likewise, I've found that when teachers can see how their teaching is changing lives, renewing minds, and making disciples, they are often transformed from lethargic volunteers into incendiary mentors.

How do I help them see the difference teaching makes?

First, I let people see flesh-and-blood proof of the transforming power of Scripture. In church services, newsletters, and worker recognition banquets, I have people report how their lives have been changed through attending a class and putting the Bible into practice. Personal testimonies, which are contemporary parables, are one of the oldest and most effective ways of casting vision.

Second, I give platforms to teachers so they can tell others what teaching has meant to them. Periodically in our church we bring a teacher forward and just say, "Tell us what's going on in your class." Once some of these teachers get warmed up, they are hard to stop, and they'll often conclude with something like, "If you're not in on this, frankly you're missing the greatest blessing in this place."

Third, I put trainees under teachers who already have passion. Never put live eggs under dead hens. Passion is more caught than taught.

Fourth, I involve trainees in actual ministry. Studying teaching in a setting detached from ministry eventually quenches passion. Passion takes root in the soil of personal experience, where a teacher can see needs up close and personal, and lives changed before their very eyes.

Some time ago I asked a layman to accompany me on a ministry trip. It occurred to me that he shouldn't be merely a spectator, so I asked him to share with the group what God had done in his life as a result of learning how to study the Scriptures for himself. He was elated. Riding home, he asked gingerly, "Do you suppose I could do that again sometime?"

Maximizing Resources

No one can train teachers effectively without drawing on other resources. Here are a few, which are occasionally neglected, that I've found helpful.

• *Proper recruiting.* Effective training starts with good recruiting. In the recruitment stage we need to avoid several approaches: (1) "I can't get anyone else to volunteer so how about you?" (2) implying that teaching requires little commitment or effort, or (3) asking people to teach as a favor to the church. These misrepresent teacher training from the start.

Instead, good recruiting conveys an exalted vision of the teaching ministry. It makes clear to volunteers that teachers are in permanent training, that a teacher is like an artist, always growing, exploring new areas of his or her potential, experimenting, fine-tuning skills. Naturally, that's the type of person ready and eager to be trained.

• *Conferences and seminars.* I have found that taking teachers to seminars enlarges their vision and equips them with skills better than anything else. In fact, a conference can do things I cannot.

When I was pastoring in Fort Worth, Texas, I once drove some teachers to a conference. Most of the way there we talked about ways to improve our Sunday school, but to most ideas, my superintendent would respond, "That's a nice idea, but it won't work in Texas."

At the conference, the superintendent attended a session taught by a man from Amarillo who advocated the very ideas we had been discussing in the car. On the drive home my superintendent spent most of the time enthusiastically telling us his "new ideas" for the Sunday school!

● *Cocoon training.* In today's cocooning culture, I've found it nearly impossible to get people out of their homes for an evening or weekend training event. But we also live in an age of audio tapes, video tapes, and literature — material that enables teachers to listen, watch, or read privately.

One surgeon, who picked up a series of audio tapes that I had recorded on the Book of James, said to me later, "Hendricks, I've listened to those tapes about twenty times, and I'm beginning to understand what you're talking about." There was no way I could have gotten this man to attend my lectures twenty times. But he did find time to hear and absorb the information when it was packaged for private consumption.

Many mothers need resources they can use after the kids go to bed. Some people prefer to learn by reading, others by listening, others by watching video tapes. The greater the diversity of resources we make available, the more likely we are to find an open door into our teachers' minds.

● *Curriculum.* One often overlooked training resource is the curriculum. Good manuals include some teacher training into each issue. I remind teachers to pay attention to this material and — like a budding artist who learns brush strokes by observing and imitating the masters — to note the various elements of the lessons themselves, how the lessons are arranged and developed.

When my son graduated from Harvard, I asked him, "Bill, how many great teachers did you have?"

He thought a while and said, "One for sure, maybe two. Although I studied under internationally known scholars, when it came to teaching skills, I felt they were missing."

At Harvard, a paragon of higher education in America, my son discovered teachers can be on the razor edge of research, can pile degrees upon degrees, but lack the ability to communicate that knowledge to the students.

If Harvard cannot assume their professors can teach well, how much less can churches. Proper training not only prevents us from producing gun-shy teachers, it also helps our teachers effectively communicate the gospel.

Mentoring is the flip side of the pastor's public roles of teacher, prophet, and priest.

— Earl Palmer

CHAPTER TWELVE

Mentoring

I remember hearing some great sermons as a youth. I recall attending some outstanding lectures at Princeton Seminary. I've been to conferences that moved me deeply. But the most important influence on my Christian life has been individuals who have mentored me.

Bob Munger, my pastor in my college days, took time to listen to me. Lynn Bolick, a classmate in seminary, helped me think through my ideas. Dale Brunner, a colleague who, when we happened to be serving Christian institutions in Manila at the same time, was a great source of encouragement.

As one who spends most of his days preaching, teaching, and administrating a church, I know the value of congregational work. But ministry to me would be pointless if, at the same time, I wasn't trying to mentor people as others have mentored me. For it's a one-on-one teaching relationship that can make the most difference.

The problem is we don't receive a lot of formal training in mentoring. Leading worship, yes. Preaching and teaching, yes. Administration and pastoral care, yes. But help in mentoring others? Not likely.

Over the years, I've reflected a lot on how others have mentored me, and I have done my share of mentoring as well. I've concluded that mentoring is the flip side of the pastor's public roles of teacher, prophet, and priest: the mentor helps the person mentored discover the truth, follow Christ's way, and know God's comfort.

Here are a few ways, then, in which I minister to individuals in my role as mentor.

Discovering the Truth

Some Christians never gain confidence in their own thoughts. They never get on with their own life because they're tied too closely to some powerful personality or dynamic leader. They're easily victimized because they're conditioned to feel they always need a strong teacher to clarify and give them truth. No one has helped them become confident enough to stand on their own.

They need to discover the kind of teacher who lives out the Hebrew word for teacher, *morah*. It comes from the same root as *torah*, "the way." A *morah* is one who teaches by pointing out the way. That's the type of teacher a mentor is: one who walks with the student part of the way, then stops and points out the rest of the journey. "You can figure it out from here," I say. "You go the rest of the way yourself."

All teachers and mentors should do at least that. But as a mentor, I want to go one step further: I want actually to learn from the person I'm mentoring. When that happens, I know I'm really mentoring, because that's when the person is really developing his or her own thoughts.

To learn from the person mentored, I have to do at least three things:

• *Stop teaching.* When I'm with an individual, I have to be cautious about dispensing information about the Bible and theology. As a pastor, I usually know much more about such things than the people I mentor. It's easy for me to slip into telling people what I've learned from a recent journal article or Bible commentary, especially after they've asked me a question about which I know something.

Although it's appropriate sometimes to give people a straight answer, most of the time I'd rather point people to the journal or commentary, summarize it, and say, "If you're really interested, why not read it. I found it helpful. I think you will too."

• *Listen.* I had just finished my first year in seminary when I went to spend a summer with Bob Munger, then pastor of First Presbyterian Church in Berkeley. With just one year of seminary under my belt, my conversations were somewhat sophomoric. Yet Bob, amazingly, seemed to enjoy hearing the little wit and wisdom this young seminarian had to offer. He actually listened to what I had to say. He made me feel like he wanted to learn from *me*!

And that's how Bob Munger became my mentor — he encouraged me to voice my own thoughts. He helped me develop because his words and posture telegraphed a vital message to me: "I respect what you say. I'm interested in your thoughts. I can learn from you."

• *Encourage disagreement.* The most effective mentors are those who are comfortable with a lively interaction with those they are mentoring. I cannot spoon feed information and be a mentor. It is when I am flexible enough to permit someone the freedom to negotiate with what I say that I mentor best.

When I was in seminary, my first roommate, Lynn Bolick, was an older senior. We got into our share of theological discussions, and we had our share of differences of opinion. But he never shut off our discussions, falling back on his extra years of education to squelch my ideas. He enjoyed the debates we entered into, and he gave me space to express myself. That process helped me clarify a great deal of my own thinking. And that, in turn, bolstered my confidence in my ability to grapple with important issues.

So I encourage the people I mentor to question what I say. After I've expressed my opinion about something, I'll say, "You'll have to sort this issue out for yourself, but that's how I see it." I might even ask if they see a problem in what I've just said.

Most important, encouraging interaction is a matter of not acting defensive when people disagree. I can't jump to defending what I've said, but instead I must listen carefully to the reply, and yes, try to learn from what the person says.

In this way, the people I'm mentoring gain confidence in their own ability to discover and understand God's Word to them. They see that I don't teach, but listen, and not just listen, but learn from them. They see that they have something significant to offer.

Discerning God's Will

In our prophetic role, pastors need to challenge people to keep the faith, fight the good fight. And often that means giving a forceful word to the congregation.

The other side of being prophetic, the side that the mentor highlights, is being an encourager. The goal is the same — living faithfully a Christian lifestyle — but the means are different: encouragement, affirmation, praise.

Again, as a mentor I don't want to tell people what God's will is for them; I want them to discover it for themselves. And that happens best, I've noticed, when I affirm what's going right with a person.

● *Express encouragement regularly.* A young lawyer in a class I taught recently wrote a paper on 1 Corinthians 15. He didn't just parrot back my lectures, however. He went beyond what I had taught, doing his own study and making his own breakthroughs. He grappled with issues we hadn't discussed in class; he dared to draw his own conclusions. It occurred to me as I read his work that I was learning from this student. So on his paper, along with his grade, I wrote a note saying his ideas had inspired me.

Sometime later he told me that little note had bolstered his confidence to work through his own thoughts and draw his own conclusions. I had confirmed that his thinking was sound, that his ideas were exciting and helpful to me. He began to have the confidence that he could teach.

I didn't plan for that one note to have that impact, but when I regularly encourage, some of my notes and words will.

● *Build trust.* People are vulnerable about things most precious to them. So poets don't want to share their poems with someone bored by poetry; musicians don't enjoy playing their compositions for someone who doesn't care for their style of music.

So I can encourage another in the things that matter only if the person will share what's important to him with me. That means I have to attend to the slow business of building trust. And that involves listening with interest to what the person shares with me and affirming the good in what they say and do.

Gradually, the person I'm mentoring will share deeper thoughts and talk about their more exciting dreams. And that's when my encouragement will really count.

● *Don't qualify the affirmation.* I meet many people who are discouraged because what personal encouragement they have received has been qualified: "Yes, that's true enough. But you forgot about this." Some have been in a Christian atmosphere where leaders always corrected them or added, "You did that well, but you also need to improve in this area."

Instead, I look for ways to give simple, direct affirmations without the "buts," without having to add anything. "You know," I'll say, "you're doing some very good thinking about this." Period. I simply affirm the people for what they're doing right. Since the people I mentor are serious about their walk with Christ, I know in most cases they'll eventually figure out where they fall short. In the meantime, I'm giving them confidence that, when they do see a shortfall, they'll be able to do something about it.

I call this kind of prophetic mentoring the ministry of agreement. The Greek word for agree is *homologea,* "to say the same word." When I agree with someone, I don't feel the need to add a single word — I say "the same word." I affirm what they've done well. This doesn't mean I never correct or take issue. It means I honor the discovery the person has made, acknowledging new footing that's been established.

● *Confront only when you've earned the right.* Naturally, as in any meaningful relationship, there comes a time when the mentor must confront the person being mentored.

For instance, I've been working with a young man for whom I have a great deal of respect. He has tremendous potential. But there is one area of his life in which he has been unrealistic: he has not been responsible in the financial support of his marriage. He's had trouble finding and keeping a job because he has set his sights way too high. His wife was supporting him and the family, but the bills kept piling up. One month recently their phone was cut off.

I had been encouraging him for months, trying to discern the direction God is calling. But at that point, if I said nothing about this problem, I would have become co-dependent to him, enabling his destructive patterns. So I had to help him see he needed to get a job: pump gas or wait on tables in a restaurant or sweep floors — anything. He needed to do something now for the sake of his wife and family, but also for himself.

I couldn't have done that at the beginning of our relationship. And I can't do that in every mentoring relationship I have — sufficient trust has not been established. But since I've been this man's friend for some time now, and since I've done nothing but encourage him up to this point, I've earned the right to tell him what I think he ought to do.

A mentor, then, offers encouragement, and sometimes direction, so that the person mentored can move ahead on his own with confidence. The goal of a mentor in medicine, for example, is to help another acquire the courage and independence of thought to do surgery alone, without needing the mentor looking over his or her shoulder. The goal in Christian mentoring is to help people discern and follow the will of God on their own.

Knowing God

The pastor as priest acts as intermediary between God and the people. At a minimum that means I pray to God for my congregation. It also means that sometimes I'm called to announce to my people God's forgiveness, in the public declaration of pardon following the confession of sins, for instance. Another priestly function is the administration of the sacraments.

The mentor's priestly function, though, is not to stand between God and the person mentored but to help the mentored person discover the comfort and forgiveness of God for himself.

This type of priestly mentoring can also take place in prayer groups. For fifteen years now I've been meeting with a group of Presbyterian pastors. We meet monthly for what we call "supportive visiting and prayer." We talk about our needs and then pray for each other. In that setting, I've often experienced the grace and comfort of God, mediated through my pastoral colleagues. In that setting, they've become priestly mentors to me, not announcing the comfort of God, but praying with me so that I might know it personally.

Beginning the Mentoring Process

Each mentoring situation is unique, but there are several things that have helped me develop meaningful relationships with those I mentor.

1. Create encounters. I can't be a mentor unless I have contact with people. So I deliberately become a part of small groups so that I might meet people whom I can mentor.

For example, I've offered a special theological study group every spring and fall throughout my ministry. For six weeks I have the chance to get close to certain people. Even though sometimes seventy or eighty people come, it still opens doors so I can get to know a few of them.

I've also been involved with a men's prayer group on Wednesday mornings. Almost weekly for nineteen years I've been able to get close to the men who attend. I also have taught annual classes at New College at Berkeley. I'll get a chance there to get to know a group of people, read their papers, and form friendships. Retreats I attend and even Sunday morning preaching may also open the door for meeting people. I watch especially for those who make the effort to make an appointment or come talk to me as a result of those encounters.

2. *Fade into the relationship.* Naturally, I can't just announce to a likely candidate, "I'm your mentor. I'm going to shape your life." Instead, I've learned I have to send signals that let a person know his life will be safe with me molding it, because in the end, it's the person who has to trust me to be a mentor.

The signals, of course, are many of the things I've mentioned above: I have to stop teaching, listen, and encourage where I see growth. When those signals are flashed time and again, the person I'm interested in mentoring begins to let me see more and more of his life.

So it's not a matter of not being a mentor one day and being a mentor the next. I didn't fully realize that Bob Munger was a mentor to me, for instance, until I looked back on my experience with him years later. Mentoring, like most relationships, is something that deepens gradually.

3. *Offer regular check ins.* Mentoring is rarely an intense relationship. I don't have a list of people I contact each week, week in and week out. It's more of a natural interaction with people when I happen to see them.

Still, I have to make the effort to stay in touch, so I want to give people opportunities to check in, to tell me how they're doing and what they're thinking about.

Although sometimes I'll set an appointment with a person, most of the time I just watch for the chance to strike up a conversation with someone after a class or meeting, for instance. That's when I'll ask, "Where are you at right now in your thinking? What can I do to help you in your journey?"

Sometimes I organize opportunities for people to check in. For instance, I regularly offer writing groups, where writers and poets share their work with each other. But I also want this to be a place where before or after and even during the meeting, individuals will briefly and informally tell me what's going in with them.

4. *Fade out of the relationship.* Mentoring is not like a therapeutic relationship. It's not seven weeks of sessions that are then terminated. I think of it more as an ongoing, highly flexible relationship, checking in with another human being, possibly for the rest of life.

There are different levels of involvement, however. And over time the intense mentoring will give way to less regular, more infrequent meetings. If I have a good mentoring relationship, even if I haven't seen the person for months, we check in with each other in a matter of minutes: I find out quickly what the person's thinking, where he's growing, where he's hurting.

Consequently, I have never become overloaded with mentoring relationships, because, while some are relatively intense for a time, they don't remain that way. There are waves of involvement, where some get a great deal of personal attention and others do not.

If I were to reduce the role of a mentor to its simplest terms, I would say a mentor is a friend. Many friends have shaped my life, though they may never have considered themselves as my mentors.

Sometimes my friends have helped me discover truth, sometimes they have encouraged me, and sometimes they have mediated the grace of God. And always, my friends valued and affirmed me. And because they did, their influence has changed me and continues to help me, even now as I mentor and influence others.

Teaching is not the mere conveying of Christian information but helping people discover for themselves the truth of the gospel.

— Mark Galli

Epilogue

As we talked with these three teachers — one woman and two men; one a graduate of Princeton Seminary, one of Fuller Seminary, one of Dallas Seminary; one a pastor, one a professor, one a college president — I was surprised to see how much they had in common. In particular, they each were concerned to highlight the following:

• Teaching is not limited to what goes on in the classroom. That only happens to be the formal and most common setting for it. But teaching also takes place in worship, in small groups, in friendships, and in casual conversation.

● Their goal is not sound teaching technique or the ability to lecture impressively. If teaching doesn't change lives, they want nothing to do with it.

● In one way or another, each describes teaching as "causing to learn." Teaching is not the mere conveying of Christian information but helping people discover for themselves the truth of the gospel.

In short, they each see teaching as a means, perhaps the principle means, of Christian discipleship. And when it's done well, what happens inside students matches the experience of the disciples on the road to Emmaus who, after having a session with the master teacher, exclaimed, "Were not our hearts burning within us while he talked with us on the road and opened the Scriptures to us?"

May such combustion continue in your teaching opportunities.